PLANE SPOTTER'S GUIDE

D0784444

OSPREY
PUBLISHING

PLANE SPOTTER'S GUIDE

Tony Holmes

First published in Great Britain in 2012 by Osprey Publishing,
PO Box 883, Oxford, OX1 9PL, UK
1385 Broadway, 5th Floor, New York, NY 10018, USA
E-mail: info@ospreypublishing.com

Osprey Publishing is part of Bloomsbury Publishing Plc

A CIP catalogue record for this book is available from the British Library.

ISBN: 978 1 78096 051 7
PDF E-Book ISBN: 978 1 78096 701 1
E-Pub ISBN: 978 1 78096 702 8

Page layout by Benedict Salvesen
Typeset in Cambria and Conduit
Originated by PDQ Digital Media Solutions
Printed in China through World Print Ltd.

16 17   11 10 9 8

The Woodland Trust
Osprey Publishing is supporting the Woodland Trust, the UK's leading woodland conservation charity,
by funding the dedication of trees.

www.ospreypublishing.com

CONVERSION TABLE	
1 millimetre (mm)	0.039in
1 centimetre (cm)	0.394in
1 metre (m)	1.094 yards
1 kilometre (km)	0.621 miles
1 kilogram (kg)	2.205lb
1 inch (in)	2.54cm
1 foot (ft)	0.305m
1 yard	0.914m
1 mile	1.61km

CONTENTS

SOPWITH PUP

Essentially a scaled-down, single-seat derivative of Sopwith's 1½ Strutter (the Royal Flying Corps' first true two-seat fighter), the much-loved Pup was initially known as the Scout. However, due to its small size and strong family resemblance to the Strutter, it was quickly dubbed the 'Pup' – an appellation that eventually became official. Ordered by both the Royal Naval Air Service (RNAS) and the Royal Flying Corps (RFC), the first Pups reached the Western Front in September 1916, and remained in frontline service until rendered obsolete by the SE 5a and the Sopwith Camel in the late summer of the following year.

The best British fighter in the frontline for more than a year, the Pup enjoyed considerable success with the various RNAS and RFC units that received examples in France and Belgium. Indeed, some 29 pilots achieved ace status with the Pup, and 22 others who claimed victories with the aircraft later 'made ace' flying Triplanes and Camels. These statistics are quite remarkable considering that the Pup units were up against deadly Albatros scouts with their twin Spandau machine guns – the Pup was armed with just a solitary Vickers gun – and far more powerful inline engines.

The key to the Pup's success was the responsiveness of its flight controls and outstanding manoeuvrability, which endeared the scout to those that flew it. Some 1,770 Pups were eventually built, and although replaced on the Western Front in the autumn of 1917, production of the fighter continued well into 1918 in order to satisfy the demand for Home Defence fighters to engage marauding German bombers and Zeppelin dirigibles.

The Pup was also a favourite with instructors at training squadrons in England, again thanks to its docile handling characteristics when compared to later fighter types such as the Camel and SE 5a. Aside from operating with RNAS units on land, a number of Pups were also embarked aboard the Royal Navy's trio of aircraft carriers from early 1917 until the war's end.

Pup N6205 of Flt Cdr J. S. T. Fall, 3 Naval
Squadron, Marieux, France, April 1917

SPECIFICATIONS (PUP)

Crew: Pilot

Length: 19ft 3.75in (5.89m)

Wingspan: 26ft 6in (8.08m)

Height: 9ft 5in (2.87m)

Empty: 787lb (357kg)

Max T/O: 1,225lb (556kg)

Max Speed: 111mph (179km/h)

Range: endurance of 3 hours

Powerplant: Le Rhône 9C

Output: 80hp (59.6kW)

Armament: One fixed Vickers 0.303in machine
gun forward of cockpit; anti-airship armament of
four Le Prieur rockets, two per interplane struts

First Flight Date: February 1916

Pup B1777 of Capt A. S. G. Lee, No 46 Sqn, Suttons Farm, Essex, August 1917

PLANE DETAILS

Previous page: Joe Fall was joint leading scorer with the Pup, and he claimed three victories with N6205 on 23 and 29 April and 1 May 1917. He had the name *BETTY* painted on the fighter's fuselage, and the aircraft also featured a red cowling and wheel covers. This 'C' Flight machine was damaged on 11 May 1917 and following repairs it served in England. Later still it became 9901 and was assigned as a ship's Pup.

This page: The colourful markings of this Pup were applied while the squadron was based at Suttons Farm, Essex, in July–August 1917 during one of the Gotha bomber scares. Arthur Gould Lee had the name *CHIN-CHOW* painted beneath the cockpit as a reference to a character in a popular London west-end show of the time. His personal markings were removed after No 46 Sqn returned to France on 30 August. Lee scored five victories with B1777 between 4 and 30 September 1917.

NIEUPORT 17

The highly successful Nieuport family of fighters were unique in their adoption of the sesquiplane wing layout, which saw them use the same wing design as a biplane, but with the lower wing possessing less than half the area of the upper flying surface. Supported by unique V-shaped interplane struts, the Gustave Delage-designed Nieuports were amongst the lightest and most manoeuvrable scouts of World War I thanks to the sesquiplane layout.

Tracing its lineage directly back to the revolutionary Nieuport 11 Bébé of early 1916, the Nieuport 17 proved to be an outstanding success, despite suffering more than its fair share of wing shedding. The most successful of all sesquiplane fighters thanks to its greater wing area and structural refinements, the 17 equipped every French *escadrille de chasse* at some point during 1916. The RFC also purchased the 17 in significant numbers, examples reaching its units in France from July 1916. The Belgian, Italian and Russian air arms also made widespread use of the 17, having operated earlier Nieuport scouts. The standard 17 enjoyed almost a year of unparalleled success in combat, effectively ending the Fokker Eindecker 'scourge' over the Western Front.

In an effort to keep the machine competitive in combat, Nieuport produced the 17bis in late 1916, this version featuring a 130hp Clerget 9B engine in place of the 110/120hp Le Rhône 9Ja/Jb that had powered the standard 17. The aircraft also boasted full-length fuselage side fairings. These modifications did very little to improve the scout's overall performance, however, and only a small number of 17bis were delivered to the French and the RNAS.

The follow-on Nieuport 23 and 24 were scarcely distinguishable from the 17, and none could match the speed and rate of climb of the SPAD series of French fighters. Nevertheless, the sesquiplanes remained in production until the end of World War I, by which time production of all Le Rhône-engined Nieuports had exceeded 7,200 aircraft.

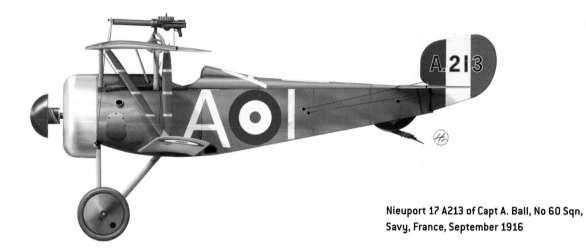

Nieuport 17 A213 of Capt A. Ball, No 60 Sqn, Savy, France, September 1916

SPECIFICATIONS
(NIEUPORT 17)

Crew: Pilot

Length: 19ft (5.80m)

Wingspan: 26ft 9in (8.16m)

Height: 7ft 10in (2.40m)

Empty: 825lb (375kg)

Max T/O: 1,232lb (560kg)

Max speed: 103mph (165km/h)

Range: endurance of 1.75 hours

Powerplant: Le Rhône 9Ja

Output: 113hp (94.2kW)

Armament: One fixed 7.7mm Vickers machine gun immediately forward of the cockpit and one moveable 7.7mm Lewis gun over the top wing

First Flight Date: January 1916

PLANE DETAILS

Previous page: A213 was received by the RFC on 3 August 1916 and transferred to No 60 Sqn on 16 September. It was assigned to 19-victory ace Capt Albert Ball, and he claimed a further 11 successes with A213 by the end of September. Note the scout's distinctive red *cône de penetration* – a hemispherical fixed fairing mounted on an extension of the stationary crankshaft. This aircraft was shot down in flames by an Albatros scout from *Jasta* 1 on 6 March 1917, killing No 60 Sqn's commanding officer, Maj E. P. Graves.

Nieuport 17 N1895 of Lt C. Nungesser,
***Escadrille* N65, Cachy, France, August 1916**

This page: The third-ranking French fighter ace of World War I with 43 victories (almost 30 of which were scored flying Nieuports), Charles Nungesser was assigned a number of scouts – including a 17bis, a 24, a 24bis and a 25 – with the serial N1895. He clearly had an affinity with this serial that verged on the superstitious, and just how he was allowed to re-mark his fighters in such a way remains a mystery. This particular aircraft was the original N1895, and it bore Nungesser's famous personal insignia on the fuselage.

ALBATROS D III

Designed to wrest from the Allies the aerial superiority gained by the Nieuport 11 Bébé and Airco DH 2 over the once all-conquering Fokker E III, the Albatros-Werke machines made their combat debut in the summer of 1916. The first of the genus, the D I and D II had an immediate impact on the air war in the autumn of that year, these fighters establishing new standards in airframe elegance. Boasting a neatly cowled 180hp Mercedes D III six cylinder inline engine and a carefully streamlined semi-monocoque wooden fuselage, the Albatros scout looked like nothing else at the front at that time. They were also the first quantity-produced fighters to mount twin-synchronised machine guns.

The D III was a further evolution of the Albatros D I/II, its chief designer, Dipl-Ing Robert Thelen, being ordered by the German *Idflieg* (*Inspektion der Fliegertruppen* – Inspectorate of Military Aviation) to abandon the solid parallel-structure single-bay wing cellule in favour of the lighter, lower-drag Nieuport-style sesquiplane cellule in an effort to make the new fighter more manoeuvrable. No fewer than 400 D IIIs were subsequently ordered by the *Idflieg* in October 1916, and production examples reached frontline *Jastas* from December of that same year.

Early D IIIs suffered from recurrent chronic wing failure in the first months of operational service due to torsional flexibility of the lower wing – reinforced wings were introduced with the second batch of 840 machines constructed by Ostdeutsche Albatros-Werke. The D III was also licence-built by Oeffag in Austria, and these machines were progressively fitted with more powerful engines that produced up to 225hp. Some 220 examples were eventually built for the Austro-Hungarians in 1917–18, and Poland procured 60 Oeffag-built machines post-war that were flown by American volunteer pilots in 1920–21. The D III eventually disappeared from service over the Western Front during 1918, but the fighter remained in the frontline with Austro-Hungarian units until the end of World War I.

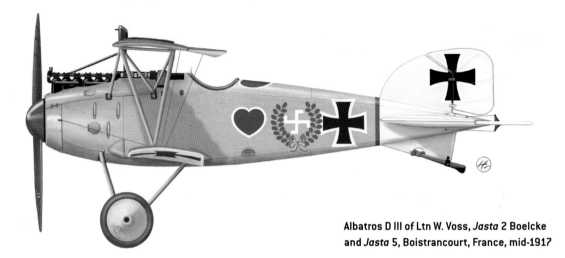

Albatros D III of Ltn W. Voss, _Jasta_ 2 Boelcke and _Jasta_ 5, Boistrancourt, France, mid-1917

SPECIFICATION (ALBATROS D III)

Crew: Pilot

Length: 24ft (7.33m)

Wingspan: 29ft 8in (9.04m)

Height: 9ft 9.25in (2.98m)

Empty: 1,457lb (661kg)

Max T/O: 1,953lb (886kg)

Max speed: 107mph (180km/h)

Range: 217 miles (350km)

Powerplant: Mercedes D IIIa

Output: 180hp (143.2kW)

Armament: Two fixed Maxim LMG 08/15 7.92mm machine guns immediately forward of the cockpit

First Flight Date: August 1916

PLANE DETAILS

Previous page:
Werner Voss, during his period with *Jasta Boelcke*, flew this much-decorated D III. When interviewed by historian Alex Imrie, Voss' motor mechanic Karl Timm recalled that the ace instructed him and Flieger Christian Rüser (the airframe mechanic) to paint a red heart with a white border on both sides of the fuselage. Then Voss had them add a white swastika (merely a good luck symbol at this time). Timm told Voss he thought this looked a bit bare, and suggested that he add a laurel wreath around the swastika, which the pilot agreed to.

Albatros D III of Ltn H. Göring, leader of *Jasta 27*, Iseghem, Belgium, June 1917

This page: Having originally flown with *Jasta* 26, Hermann Göring became leader of *Jasta* 27 in mid-May 1917. He flew this Albatros D III during his early period with the unit, the fighter being predominantly decorated with black and white paint – the most common colours held in *Jasta* stores at this time. Göring had brought this aircraft with him from *Jasta* 26, where it had worn different markings. The D III was written off on 16 July 1917.

15

SPAD VII

The end result of the design trend of 1915–16 that saw heavier, more powerful and less agile fighting scouts appearing from the warring nations of Europe, the SPAD VII was easily the most successful aircraft of this period to emerge from France. Powered by the superb, but often temperamental, Hispano-Suiza V8 engine, the 150hp SPAD VII prototype flew for the first time in April 1917. Designed by Louis Béchereau of the *Société anonyme pour l'Aviation et ses Dérivés* (SPAD), the aircraft had an impressive top speed both in level flight and in a dive, but lacked the manoeuvrability of contemporary Nieuports. However, combat reports received from the front suggested that pilots valued high speed over agility, hence the heavy fighter route chosen by SPAD.

Production examples began reaching French combat units in the summer of 1916, but the delivery tempo was slow due to production difficulties with the scout's V8 engine. The SPAD VII entered combat with both the French *Aviation Militaire* and the RFC at much the same time, and once its engine maladies

had been rectified the fighter enjoyed great success over the Western Front.

Armed with a single 7.7mm Vickers machine gun offset to the right above the engine, the SPAD VII soon made its mark in the skies over France and Belgium in the hands of aces such as Armand Pinsard, Paul Sauvage and Georges Guynemer. Indeed, the latter pilot was so taken by the fighter that he dubbed it the 'flying machine gun'. Most French *escadrille de chasse* flew the SPAD VII at some stage in World War I, and the aircraft also saw considerable action with Belgian, Italian, American and Russian units during the conflict. By the time production of the SPAD VII ended in the final months of 1918, around 6,000 examples had been built and Allied aces on every front had enjoyed success with the aircraft.

"Vieux Charles"

SPAD VII S115 of Sgt G. Guynemer, *Escadrille* N3, Cachy, France, September 1916

SPECIFICATIONS (SPAD VII)

Crew: Pilot

Length: 19ft 11.3in (6.08m)

Wingspan: 25ft 8in (7.82m)

Height: 7ft 2.75in (2.20m)

Empty: 1,102lb (500kg)

Max T/O: 1,552lb (704kg)

Max Speed: 132mph (212 km/h)

Range: endurance of 1.85 hours

Powerplant: Hispano-Suiza HS 8Ab

Output: 180hp (134kW)

Armament: One fixed Vickers 7.7mm machine gun forward of cockpit

First Flight Date: April 1916

PLANE DETAILS

Previous page: The most revered of all French aces, Georges Guynemer was a great proponent of the SPAD fighter. S115 was the first SPAD VII to be issued to him, the fighter arriving at Cachy on 27 August 1916. He claimed four victories with the scout between 4 and 23 September. S115 was brought down in error by a French 75mm shell on the latter date shortly after Guynemer had despatched a pair of Fokker scouts. Although injured when the fighter crashed, the ace acknowledged that he had only survived because of the SPAD's rugged structure.

This page: This aircraft was assigned to United States Air Service ace Capt Bill Thaw on 27 February 1918, the pilot claiming two scouts and a balloon destroyed in S5301 between 27 March and 20 April. It was decorated with the famous *Lafayette* Sioux head insignia that adorned all 103rd Aero Squadron aircraft, as well as Thaw's 'T' monogram. Also flown by Thaw's squadronmates 1Lts Hobart Baker and Drummond Cannon, S5301 was retired by the unit on 16 June 1918.

SOPWITH CAMEL

The most famous British fighting scout of World War I, the Sopwith Camel was also the most successful design to see service with either side in respect to the number of victories claimed by its pilots – 1,294 aeroplanes (including, controversially, the 'Red Baron' himself, Rittmeister Manfred Freiherr von Richthofen) and three airships destroyed.

Designed by Herbert Smith following his success with the Pup and Triplane, the Camel was the first purpose-built British fighter to boast two Vickers machine guns synchronised to fire through the propeller arc. The humped fairing covering the breeches of these weapons actually provided the inspiration for the fighter's unique sobriquet, which, like its predecessor the Pup, went from being an unofficial appellation to its official name.

Although the Camel boasted a fearsome reputation in combat, the fighter's exacting handling characteristics took a heavy toll on poorly trained novice pilots. Sensitivity, skill and experience were needed to master the Camel, which had a tendency to drop its nose during a steep turn to starboard (the direction in which its large, weighty rotary engine was spinning). It also rose alarmingly with a port climbing turn (against the direction of the rotary engine, which spun around with the propeller). In both cases the pilot had to apply liberal amounts of left rudder to retain control of the scout.

Nevertheless, near on 5,500 Camels were eventually built, the Sopwith design seeing service not only with the RNAS, RFC and the Royal Air Force (RAF) on the Western and Italian fronts, but also with Home Defence units in the nightfighter role, at sea with the RNAS in specially modified form and with two squadrons of the United States Air Service in France. A total of 2,519 F 1 and 129 2F 1 Camels were on RAF charge on 31 October 1918, but these were quickly replaced by the similar Sopwith Snipe in the months after the Armistice came into effect.

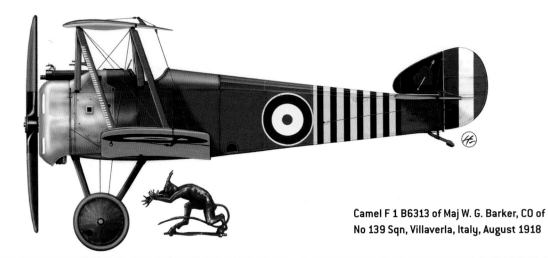

Camel F 1 B6313 of Maj W. G. Barker, CO of
No 139 Sqn, Villaverla, Italy, August 1918

SPECIFICATIONS
(CAMEL F 1)

Crew: Pilot

Length: 18ft 9in (5.72m)

Wingspan: 28ft (8.53m)

Height: 8ft 6in (2.59m)

Empty: 929lb (421kg)

Max T/O: 1,453lb (659kg)

Max Speed: 113mph (182km/h)

Range: endurance of 2.5 hours

Powerplant: Clerget 9B

Output: 130hp (96.6kW)

Armament: Two fixed Vickers 0.303in machine
guns forward of cockpit; optional underwing
racks for four 25lb (11.3kg) bombs

First Flight Date: 22 December 1916

PLANE DETAILS

Camel F 1 B6358 of Flt Sub-Lt L. P. Coombes, 10 Naval Squadron, Treizennes, France, spring 1918

Previous page:

The most famous and highest scoring Camel of them all, Maj Barker's F 1 B6313 served with him in Nos 45, 66 and, finally, 139 Sqns. Between 20 October 1917 and 18 September 1918 the Canadian ace claimed 46 aerial victories on the Western and Italian fronts in this long-lived machine. Note the white 'notch' markings painted on the fighter's forward interplane strut, denoting each of Barker's victories, and the flat metal red devil attached to the starboard gun that acted as a foresight for the pilot.

This page: It was in the B6358 that Lawrence Coombes gained his first two victories. The aircraft had previously seen action with the Seaplane Defence Flight, where Flt Sub-Lt J. E. Greene had destroyed a balloon with it. Transferred to 'Naval 9', the Camel had been used by Flt Sub-Lt M. S. Taylor to drive down a DFW in January 1918. Following its spell with 'Naval 10', B6358 went to No 213 Sqn. Here, Lt G. D. Smith shared a victory while flying the aircraft on 7 July. The scout was lost in action on 25 August 1918.

RAF SE 5/5a

Undoubtedly one of the best British fighters of World War I, the SE 5/5a was easily the most successful aircraft designed by the Royal Aircraft Factory (RAF) at Farnborough. Although less nimble than its frontline contemporary, the Sopwith Camel, the SE 5a enjoyed the inherent stability of all previous RAF designs, thus making it easier to fly. It could out-dive and out-climb the Camel, sustain more combat damage and yet remain intact despite performing high-g manoeuvres. The aircraft's only failing centred on its original powerplant, the Hispano-Suiza 8A engine. This suffered from chronic unreliability, and these problems were only solved when the Wolseley direct-drive W 4a Viper was introduced as a replacement engine. This too endured its fair share of teething troubles, but these were eventually overcome.

The SE 5a was developed from the original SE 5, which entered frontline service in March 1917 with No 56 Sqn – this ultimately became a crack unit in the RFC/RAF, having produced no fewer than 26 aces and downed 401 enemy aircraft by the end of World War I. The improved SE 5a reached the RFC in June 1917, the aircraft now having a more powerful 200hp Hispano-Suiza 8B engine fitted in place of the troublesome 150hp unit from the same company. It soon became a firm favourite amongst the leading British and Empire aces of the war. Indeed, James McCudden, Mick Mannock, Anthony Beauchamp Proctor and George McElroy would all claim more than 40 aerial victories whilst at the controls of a SE 5/5a.

A total of 22 squadrons in the RAF, Australian Flying Corps and US Air Service were equipped with the SE 5a on the Western Front when Germany surrendered in November 1918, some 5,125 examples of the fighting scout having been built in just 18 months by five companies in the UK. Like the Camel, the SE 5a did not survive long in the peacetime RAF. Small numbers saw service in Canada and Australia, however, and more than 60 SE 5as were built for US Army use from components in 1919.

SE 5a D3511 of Maj R. S. Dallas, No 40 Sqn, Bruay, France, May 1918

SPECIFICATIONS (SE 5a)

Crew: Pilot

Length: 20ft 11in (6.38m)

Wingspan: 26ft 11in (8.11m)

Height: 9ft 6in (2.89m)

Empty: 1,531lb (694kg)

Max T/O: 2,048lb (929kg)

Max Speed: 120mph (193km/h)

Range: endurance of 2.25 hours

Powerplant: Hispano-Suiza 8B or Wolseley W 4a Viper

Output: 200hp (149.3kW)

Armament: One fixed Vickers 0.303in machine gun on port fuselage side and one Lewis 0.303in machine gun on Foster mount on upper wing; bomb load of 100lb (44kg) on fuselage racks

First Flight Date: 22 November 1916 (SE 5)

SE 5a C1149 of Capt D. W. Grinnell-Milne,
Le Hameau, France, January 1919

PLANE DETAILS

Previous page: Australian ace Maj Roderic Dallas flew D3511 during his two-month tenure as CO of No 40 Sqn in 1918, and he claimed at least five victories with it in May. The aircraft boasted a decidedly non-standard camouflage scheme devoid of unit markings that had almost certainly been applied in the field by No 40 Sqn. Fellow aces captains Gwilym Lewis and George McElroy flew D3511 following Dallas' death in action on 1 June, Lewis claiming two victories with it in early July.

This page: C1149 was delivered to No 56 Sqn on 21 October 1918 and used by Capt Duncan Grinnell-Milne to claim his sixth victory (a Fokker D VII) on 3 November. Following the cessation of hostilities, Grinnell-Milne had an unpainted spinner fitted and the nickname *Schweinhund* applied in white on the nose. The entire fuselage and tailplane were painted red, as was the propeller boss, which also boasted thin white borders. Grinnell-Milne eventually flew this machine from Le Hameau for disposal on 23 January 1919.

FOKKER Dr I

Without a doubt the most famous fighter type to see service on either side during World War I, the Fokker Dr I was inspired by the Sopwith Triplane of 1916–17. Boasting three superimposed wings, the British scout enjoyed much better manoeuvrability than any other fighter then in service over the Western Front, and the small number flown by the RNAS scored many kills over its German Albatros and Fokker rivals. In response, the Fokker *Flugzeugwerke* devised the *Dreidecker* (hence 'Dr'), which made its first flight in June 1917. A trio of pre-production F Is were built in August and single examples supplied to leading aces Rittmeister Manfred Freiherr von Richthofen and Leutnant Werner Voss. Their exploits with these aircraft in the autumn of 1917 quickly created a myth of invincibility surrounding the Fokker triplane that preceded the Dr I's introduction to service in October of that year.

Rittmeister von Richthofen was so impressed with the triplane's performance that he wrote in his diary 'It climbed like a monkey and was as manoeuvrable as the devil'. His enthusiastic support for the Fokker fighter ensured that his *Jagdgeschwader* Nr I, known as the 'Flying Circus', was the first unit to completely re-equip with the new fighter, and in the skilled hands of its numerous aces, the Dr I proved a formidable opponent.

Wing failures plagued the revolutionary fighter throughout its brief career in the frontline, and the aircraft was temporarily grounded in November 1917. The faulty wings were quickly strengthened, and the Dr I remained in service on the Western Front until replaced by the superior Fokker D VII from May 1918. Just weeks prior to that, however, Germany's leading ace, the great 'Red Baron', had been killed at the controls of a Dr I on the morning of 21 April 1918. Ultimately, only 320 triplanes would be built, yet the fighter has come to symbolise the exploits of World War I's 'Knights of the Air' more than any other aircraft from this period.

Fokker Dr I 425/17 of Rittmeister Manfred von Richthofen,
JG I, Cappy, France, April 1918

SPECIFICATIONS
(FOKKER Dr I)

Crew: Pilot

Length: 18ft 11in (5.77m)

Wingspan: 23ft 7.5in (7.17m)

Height: 9ft 8in (2.95m)

Empty: 904lb (410kg)

Max T/O: 1,289lb (585kg)

Max speed: 103mph (165km/h)

Range: endurance of 1.5 hours

Powerplant: Obursel Ur II

Output: 110hp (96.6kW)

Armament: Two fixed Maxim LMG 08/15 7.92mm machine guns immediately forward of the cockpit

First Flight Date: June 1917

PLANE DETAILS

Previous page: Manfred von Richthofen's Dr I 425/17 (Wk-Nr 2009) was one of the few aircraft that the Rittmeister flew that was actually all red – the smooth finish evident in photographs suggests it may have been painted this way at the factory. The aircraft is seen here as it appeared on 21 April 1917, when World War I's 'ace of aces' was shot down and killed chasing his 81st victory.

Fokker Dr I 450/17 of Ltn J. Jacobs, *Jasta 7*, St Marguerite, France, May 1918

This page: Josef Jacobs claimed 47 or 48 victories, with as many as 30 of these being achieved at the controls of a Dr I. This made him the leading Fokker triplane ace of the war. The last operational Dr Is were two aircraft assigned to *Jasta* 7 and flown exclusively by Jacobs, 450/17 being one of these machines – he used it from March until the aircraft was shot down by an SE 5as while Jacobs was defending *Jasta* 7's St Marguerite airfield on 3 October 1918.

FOKKER D VII

Created by Fokker's highly talented design team, the prototype D VII was completed in great haste in late 1917 so that it could enter the German D-Type standard fighter competition held at Adlershof in January/February 1918. Emerging the clear winner, the D VII design boasted a simple, yet strong, welded-steel tube fuselage and cantilever wing cellule. It was put into widespread production by Fokker, and licences were obtained by Albatros and its subsidiary OAW.

Once committed to frontline service with *Jagdgeschwader* I in May 1918, the D VII proved to be the best fighting scout in service with either side. Indeed, it was claimed that the Fokker could make a good pilot into an ace, and it set the standards against which all new fighters were measured for more than a decade. The key to the D VII's success was its controllability, as although it was not the fastest fighter on the Western Front during the summer and autumn of 1918, nor was it the most manoeuvrable, it was certainly the most effective in combat.

An outstandingly easy aeroplane to fly, the D VII was forgiving, yet extraordinarily responsive. Its stall was straightforward to correct and it was a reluctant spinner. The fighter also remained fully under control when its opponents (especially the Camel) stalled and spun away. Finally, and most importantly, the D VII was a stable gun platform.

Available in significant quantities in the final six months of the war, D VIIs (both Mercedes D IIIaü and BMW IIIa powered versions) equipped not only myriad army *Jagdstaffeln* but also home defence units and German Navy *Marine Feld Jastas* in Flanders. Precise production figures for the D VII have been lost, but it is thought that somewhere in the region of 3,200 were ordered and 2,000+ delivered before the Armistice. Proof of the fighter's formidable reputation came when the victorious Allies specifically stated in the surrender terms dictated to Germany that all surviving D VIIs had to be handed over.

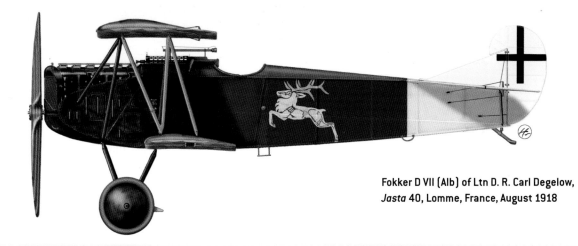

Fokker D VII (Alb) of Ltn D. R. Carl Degelow,
Jasta 40, Lomme, France, August 1918

SPECIFICATIONS
(FOKKER D VII)

Crew: Pilot

Length: 22ft 9.66in (6.95m)

Wingspan: 29ft 2.333in (8.90m)

Height: 9ft (2.75m)

Empty: 1,508lb (604kg)

Max T/O: 2,006lb (910kg)

Max speed: 116mph (187km/h)

Range: endurance of 1.5 hours

Powerplant: Mercedes D IIIaü

Output: 180hp (134kW)

Armament: Two fixed Maxim LMG 08/15 7.92mm machine guns immediately forward of the cockpit

First Flight Date: December 1917

Fokker D VII of Off-Stv W. Kühne, *Jasta* 18, Möntingen, France, August 1918

PLANE DETAILS

Previous page: *Jasta* 40's D VIIs all sported black fuselages, augmented by a white tail unit. Cabane and landing gear struts and wheel covers were also black. The wings of this Albatros-built D VII are covered in five-colour fabric, with blue rib tapes and a diagonal white stripe on the top wing to identify the *Staffelführer*. Degelow's 'white stag' emblem displays golden yellow antlers and hooves. One of the leading D VII aces, Degelow claimed at least 24 of his 30 victories with the Fokker.

This page: The red and white Fokker D VIIs of *Jasta* 18 were amongst the most strikingly marked fighters on the Western Front during the last year of the war. This particular machine was flown occasionally by D VII ace Wilhelm Kühne, who claimed all seven of his confirmed victories (four of them were balloons) with *Jasta* 18 between 25 March and 28 August 1918. He was killed on 30 August attacking RAF DH 9s of No 55 Sqn.

POLIKARPOV I-16

The world's first cantilever low wing monoplane and retractable undercarriage fighter to enter frontline service, the I-16 was an incredibly advanced design for its time. However, by the outbreak of World War II, it had been well and truly left behind by more modern fighter types. Despite this fact, the I-16 still equipped two-thirds of all Soviet Army air force fighter units when Germany invaded in June 1941. Indeed, as a sign of just how revered the I-16 was in the USSR, although production had been stopped in 1940, Polikarpov was ordered to re-open the line just 12 months later!

The first I-16s had entered service in the Soviet Union in early 1935, the fighter being powered by a reverse-engineered Wright Cyclone (designated the Shvetsov M-25). Throughout its long production life the aircraft was periodically upgraded through the fitment of uprated Shvetsov engines and improved armament. The I-16 initially saw action with the Republican forces in the Spanish Civil War, some 278 being supplied by the USSR. It was here that the aircraft's outstanding manoeuvrability was first used to telling effect. The I-16's ailerons were feather light, it boasted an exceptional roll rate and the fighter possessed excellent zoom climb ability. Offsetting these positives was the fact that the I-16 was only a satisfactory gun platform due to its oversensitivity to control movements.

Nevertheless, the I-16 was the primary Soviet fighter during the Nomonhan Incident with Japan in 1939, where it suffered terribly at the hands of the more agile Ki-27 and A5M. Later that same year the I-16 bore the brunt of the fighting with Finland in the Winter War of 1939–40, before being thrown into the fray against the Luftwaffe in June 1941. Despite suffering staggering losses in these conflicts, the I-16 still produced a large number of ace pilots with five or more aerial victories claimed whilst flying the Polikarpov fighter. The I-16 was finally retired from frontline service in 1943.

I-16 Type 5 of 5 *Escuadrilla/Grupo de Caza*,
Spain, late 1937

SPECIFICATIONS
(I-16 TYPE 10)

Crew: Pilot

Length: 19ft 11.15in (6.07m)

Wingspan: 29ft 6.33in (9m)

Height: 8ft 4.75in (2.56m)

Empty: 2,976lb (1,350kg)

Max T/O: 3,781lb (1,715kg)

Max Speed: 273mph (440km/h)

Range: 497 miles (800km)

Powerplant: Shvetsov M-25A

Output: 750hp (578kW)

Armament: Two 7.62mm machine guns in nose and two in wings; provision for six underwing 82mm rockets or up to 441lb (200kg) bombs under wings

First Flight Date: 31 December 1933

I-16 Type 24 of Sgt G. Guryanov, 4th GIAP,
Baltic Fleet Air Force, Leningrad Front, USSR,
spring 1942

PLANE DETAILS

Previous page: This fighter's standard camouflage scheme was applied at Factory No 21 at Nizhniy Novgorod, although the engine cowling and spinner were probably painted black during its service in the Soviet Union – many of the I-16s supplied to the Republicans had seen previous service with the Red Air Force. The fighter may well have been flown by Soviet pilots prior to its capture when Nationalist forces overran its unidentified base at the end of 1937.

This page: A temporary white winter camouflage scheme using lime-based paint has been applied to this aircraft, which was flown by Sgt (later Snr Lt) Grigoriy Guryanov. Prior to moving on to the La-5 in 1943, Guryanov scored four individual and three shared victories with the I-16 out of an overall total of seven individual and three shared victories. Guryanov perished on 25 August 1944 when his fighter was shot down by German flak.

BOEING B-17 FLYING FORTRESS

Built as a private venture by Boeing in response to a US Army Air Corps (USAAC) requirement for an anti-shipping bomber replacement for the Martin B-10, the Model 299 was first flown on 28 July 1935. The first four-engined bomber ever built by Boeing, the Model 299 was a huge financial risk for the company. Immediately dubbed the 'Flying Fortress' by the press corps in attendance for the prototype's first flight, the aircraft impressed the USAAC with its speed and high altitude performance. However, it was not initially chosen to replace the B-10 on the grounds of cost.

Nevertheless, the Model 229 had elicited enough interest for Boeing to receive an order for a batch of 13 YB-17s, followed by the signing of a second contract for 39 near-identical B-17Bs. The latter model introduced a new nose and bigger rudder and flaps, and the aircraft that entered service in 1939–40 looked similar to the thousands of Flying Fortresses which would subsequently dominate the ranks of the US Army Air Force (USAAF) in World War II.

By mid-1940 the Flying Fortress had been further improved with the addition of two extra guns and the fitment of more powerful engines. Designated the B-17C, 20 were exported to Britain for service with the RAF. Lessons learned from the European conflict saw Boeing 'beef up' the armour fitted to future models of B-17, plus fit extra guns and self-sealing fuel tanks. The result of these changes was the B-17E, 512 of which were built in 1941–42, followed by the B-17F, which had a redesigned nose to incorporate a 0.50in machine gun, a strengthened undercarriage to cope with increased bomb loads and Wright R-1820-97 engines. The final version to see mass-production was the chin-turreted B-17G, some 8,680 examples of which were manufactured from 1942 through to 1945. Although both E- and F-models had experienced combat with bomb groups both in the Pacific and Europe, it was the B-17G that really took the fight to the Axis on a global scale. The Flying Fortresses also saw limited service in specialised air-sea rescue and transport roles post-war.

B-17E-BO 41-9019 of the 414th BS/97th BG, Polebrook, Northamptonshire, September 1942

SPECIFICATIONS (B-17G)

Crew: Pilot and co-pilot, flight engineer, navigator, bombardier/nose gunner, radio operator/dorsal gunner, two waist gunners, ball turret gunner and tail gunner

Length: 74ft 4in (22.66m)

Wingspan: 103ft 9in (31.62m)

Height: 19ft 1in (5.82m)

Empty: 36,135lb (16,391kg)

Max T/O: 65,500lb (29,710kg)

Max Speed: 287mph (462km/h)

Range: 2,000 miles (3,219km)

Powerplant: four Wright R-1820-97 Cyclones

Output: 4,800hp (3,580kW)

Armament: Twin Browning 0.50in machine guns in chin, dorsal, ball and tail turrets, plus two in nose, one in radio compartment and one in each waist position; maximum bomb load of 12,800lb (5,800kg) in bomb-bay

First Flight Date: 28 July 1935 (Model 299)

B-17G-35-VE 42-97880 of the 324th BS/91st BG,
Bassingbourn, Cambridgeshire, September 1944

PLANE DETAILS

Previous page: Seen here in its RAF bomber colour scheme (bar the Boeing-applied sky blue, which was painted out with USAAF grey), this aircraft was assigned to the US 414th Bombardment Squadron (BS) in March 1942 and arrived in the UK with the unit four months later. Transferred to the 305th Bombardment Group (BG) on 6 November 1942, it was passed on to the 381st BG in June 1943, the 92nd BG the following month and, finally, the 482nd BG in August 1943. 41-9019 remained with the latter unit until written off two years later.

This page: Assigned to the 91st BG in June 1944 upon its arrival in the UK, this aircraft was badly damaged when it took a direct flak hit over Cologne on 15 October. The bomber had to be cut in two and a replacement rear section (from 42-31405) grafted on. The 'new' 42-97880 suffered a crash-landing on 4 April 1945, the bomber being transferred to the 306th BG after being repaired. Surviving the war, the veteran B-17 was eventually scrapped in the UK.

BRISTOL BLENHEIM

The Blenheim was the result of a speculative private venture on the part of the manufacturer, Bristol. Unencumbered by restrictions on the aircraft's weight, powerplants, general layout or radius of action, the Bristol design team produced a sleek twin-engined machine known as the Type 142. First flown at Filton on 12 April 1935, the aircraft's performance sent ripples through the RAF when it was discovered that its top speed was 30mph greater than Fighter Command's then new biplane fighter, the Gloster Gauntlet I. The Air Ministry ordered 150 airframes, which they christened Blenheim Is, and the first of these entered service with the RAF in March 1937.

By September 1939 most UK-based Blenheim squadrons had replaced their Mk Is with the improved Mk IV, the latter having grown out of an Air Ministry requirement for a reconnaissance type with greater crew accommodation and an increased range. The backbone of Bomber Command at the start of hostilities, the Mk IV made both the first armed reconnaissance incursion into German airspace (on 3 September 1939) and the first bombing raid on German targets (24 hours later). Over the next three years Blenheim crews first struggled to stem the tide of the *Blitzkrieg* in the Low Countries, and then attempted to take the war to German forces in occupied Europe in the first Channel sweeps, which resulted in alarming losses. Overseas, the story was little better as Blenheims fell like flies to Axis fighters in North Africa, the Mediterranean and the Far East.

The Blenheim was also pressed into service by Fighter Command, the modified aircraft boasting four Browning 0.303in machine guns in a pack beneath the fuselage. Designated the Mk IF, it enjoyed little success during daylight hours, but was soon modified into a promising nightfighter when fitted with the first airborne radar sets.

Despite its shortcomings, the Blenheim, in various marks, remained in the frontline well into 1943 in North Africa and the Far East.

**Blenheim IV N6181 of No 101 Sqn,
West Raynham, Norfolk, August 1940**

SPECIFICATIONS
(BLENHEIM IV)

Crew: Pilot, navigator/bomb aimer and turret gunner

Length: 42ft 7in (12.98m)

Wingspan: 56ft 4in (17.17m)

Height: 9ft 10in (3m)

Empty: 9,790lb (4,441kg)

Max T/O: 14,400lb (6,532kg)

Max Speed: 266mph (428km/h)

Range: 1,460 miles (2,350km)

Powerplant: two Bristol Mercury XVs

Output: 1,810hp (1,350kW)

Armament: One fixed Browning 0.303in machine gun in port wing and one in dorsal turret; maximum bomb load of 1,320lb (600kg) in bomb-bay

First Flight Date: 12 April 1935

Blenheim IF K7159 of No 54 OTU,
Church Fenton, North Yorkshire, September 1941

PLANE DETAILS

Previous page: Built by Bristol in Filton during the summer of 1939, N6181 was initially delivered to No 107 Sqn before being passed on to No 35 Sqn. The aircraft was then assigned to No 101 Sqn, which flew operational attacks against the German invasion barges in the Channel ports from July 1940. N6181 spent only a short time with the squadron before joining No 13 Operational Training Unit (OTU). It was struck off charge following an accident on 3 October 1940.

This page: Built as a Blenheim I bomber in late 1937, this aircraft was issued new to No 61 Sqn in January 1938. It was then converted into a Mk IF fighter through the fitment of an underfuselage gun pack and assigned to Fighter Command's Nos 222 and 145 Sqns in 1939–40. Relegated to No 5 OTU in April 1940, K7159 served with a series of Training Command units until it hit a tree and crashed during a night landing on 6 May 1943.

CONSOLIDATED PBY CATALINA

It is extremely unlikely that the PBY Catalina's record of being the most extensively built flying boat in aviation history will ever be surpassed. Consolidated constructed (or granted licences to build in Canada, where the PBY was called the Canso, and the USSR) more than 4,000 examples of the robustly simple twin-engined, high-winged aircraft over a ten-year period starting in 1935. Used by virtually all the Allied nations during World War II, the humble PBY flew more hours on combat patrols than any other American warplane of the period.

The US Navy's VP-11F was the first unit to receive the new flying boat, taking on strength its premier PBY-1 in October 1936. Such was the pace of re-equipment that by mid-1938 14 patrol squadrons were operating PBYs, and many more were scheduled to receive them. In those days, when radar and satellite reconnaissance had not yet even been dreamt of, long-ranging patrol flying boats were the only means available to solve the US Pacific and Atlantic Fleets' scouting problems.

Further improvements to the engine specification resulted in new variants entering service over the next four years, with the PBY-5A of December 1939 finally introducing the tricycle undercarriage, and thus making it a far more versatile design. Consolidated continued to update, re-engine and generally improve its tried and trusted PBY throughout the years of conflict, the final wartime variant being the PBY-6A, (designated the OA-10B in USAAF service). By then the RAF had been operating the PBY for six years, having christened the flying boat Catalina – a name officially adopted in the USA in 1942.

The final American-built PBYs were delivered as late as December 1945, and a significant number of Catalinas remained in military service across the globe well into the 1970s. The flying boat also found post-war employment in civilian hands as a fire-bomber, serving in this role in North America and Europe for many years.

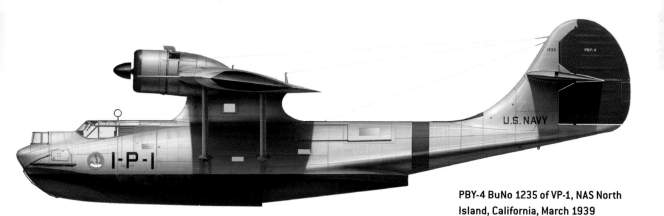

PBY-4 BuNo 1235 of VP-1, NAS North Island, California, March 1939

SPECIFICATIONS (PBY-5A)

Crew: Pilot and co-pilot, flight engineer, radar/radio operator, navigator, nose gunner, two beam gunners

Length: 63ft 10.50in (19.47m)

Wingspan: 104ft (31.70m)

Height: 20ft 2in (6.50m)

Empty: 20,910lb (9,485kg)

Max T/O: 35,420lb (16,066kg)

Max speed: 179mph (288km/h)

Range: 2,545 miles (4,096km)

Powerplant: two Pratt & Whitney R-1830-92 Twin Wasps

Output: 2,400hp (1,790kW)

Armament: One Browning 0.30/0.50in machine gun in nose, each waist blister and in 'tunnel' behind hull step; maximum bomb/mine/torpedo load of 2,000lb (907kg) on underwing racks

First Flight Date: 21 March 1935

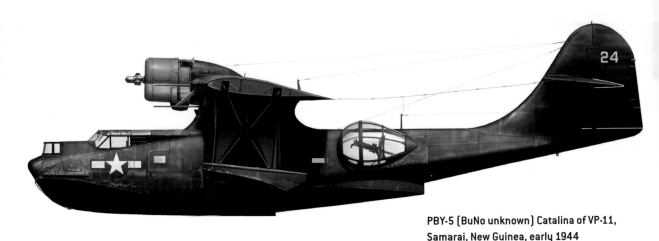

PBY-5 (BuNo unknown) Catalina of VP-11, Samarai, New Guinea, early 1944

PLANE DETAILS

Previous page: One of 19 PBY-4s assigned to VP-1, this aircraft was delivered to the unit on 19 January 1939 from Consolidated. VP-1 became VP-21 on the eve of its return to Pearl Harbor on 1 July, and BuNo 1235 completed the trip between Hawaii and the Philippines three times during the Neutrality Patrol in September 1939. It later served with VP-102 in the Dutch East Indies during 1941–42. BuNo 1235 suffered mechanical failure in flight in January 1942 and crashed in the surf off a Timor beach.

This page: Used for attacking Japanese troops and transport moving under the cover of darkness, this anonymous VP-11 PBY-5 'Black Cat' featured cowlings from a conventionally painted Catalina when it received replacement Pratt & Whitney R-1830-92s during an overhaul. The Twin Wasp was a fine engine, but after some 300 to 400 flying hours they would need a thorough overhaul. Maintenance crews in-theatre, functioning with a minimum of gear, did this job well … and often.

MESSERSCHMITT Bf 109

Numerically the most abundant fighter produced by either side during World War II, the Messerschmitt Bf 109 was to form the backbone of the *Jagdwaffe* on both the Eastern and Western Fronts, as well as in the Mediterranean and North Africa. The original Dipl-Ing Willy Messerschmitt-designed Bf 109 V1 flew for the first time on 28 May 1935, powered by a 695hp Rolls-Royce Kestrel engine. By the time fighters were issued to the Luftwaffe in the spring of 1937, the Bf 109 had been re-engined with the Junkers Jumo 210 inline powerplant. Another 18 months, and two sub-types, were to pass before the originally specified Daimler-Benz DB 601 engine was made available in sufficient quantities to allow Messerschmitt to commit the outstanding E-model to production in mid-1938. From that moment on, the Bf 109 and the DB 600 series engine would prove to be inseparable.

From the first hours of the *Blitzkrieg* in Poland on 1 September 1939, the Bf 109E was charged with securing aerial supremacy over the marauding Wehrmacht. However, as good as it was, the *Emil* was being progressively bettered in virtually all aspects of aerial combat by the Spitfire as 1941 progressed, so Messerschmitt produced the F-model, with its more aerodynamically refined nose contours covering the uprated DB 601E engine. Over an 18-month period, more than 2,000 were built, before production switched to the most durable and most populous (more than 30,000 constructed) of all Bf 109s, the *Gustav*.

Designed around the 1,475hp DB 605 engine, the G-model introduced cockpit pressurisation – crucial from late 1942 onwards when the fighter *Gruppen* struggled to repel high-altitude USAAF daylight bomber raids. A variety of integral and podded machine guns and cannon of various calibre were made available for use with the *Gustav*, as were unguided rockets and mortars. Despite the advent of better fighters, the Bf 109G and the near-identical K-model still remained a perfectly good aircraft when flown to their strengths right up to VE-Day.

Bf 109E-4 Wk-Nr 5344 of Hauptmann H. Wick,
Gruppenkommandeur of I./JG 2 'Richthofen',
Beaumont-le-Roger, France, October 1940

SPECIFICATIONS
(Bf 109G-6)

Crew: Pilot

Length: 29ft 7.5in (9.03m)

Wingspan: 32ft 6.5in (9.92m)

Height: 8ft 2.5in (2.50m)

Empty: 5,893lb (2,673kg)

Max T/O: 7,496lb (3,400kg)

Max Speed: 386mph (621km/h)

Range: 620 miles (998km) with external tank

Powerplant: Daimler-Benz DB 605AM

Output: 1,800hp (1,342kW)

Armament: One 20mm cannon in propeller hub and two 13mm machine guns in upper cowling, with option of two 20mm cannon in pods under wings; provision for various underfuselage and underwing stores

First Flight Date: 28 May 1935 (Bf 109 V1)

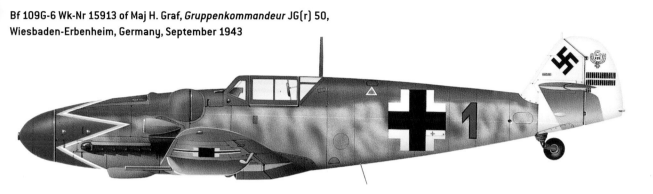

Bf 109G-6 Wk-Nr 15913 of Maj H. Graf, *Gruppenkommandeur* JG(r) 50, Wiesbaden-Erbenheim, Germany, September 1943

PLANE DETAILS

Previous page: Unlike many *Jagdflieger* in 1940, Helmut Wick retained the same aircraft throughout most of the latter part of his brief, but illustrious, career. Here, his Bf 109E-4 Wk-Nr 5344 sports *Gruppenkommandeur's* chevrons. Note also the *Staffel* badge for 3./JG 2 on the cowling and the *Geschwader* badge beneath the windscreen. On 28 November 1940, Wick (then the Luftwaffe's ranking ace with 56 kills) was himself shot down south of the Isle of Wight in this aircraft. Although he parachuted into the Channel, not trace of him was ever found.

This page: This G-6 'Kanonenboot' was the mount of Hermann Graf during his tenure of office as *Kommandeur* of JG(r) 50. The rudder meticulously records all of Graf's Eastern Front victories, the number 172 (for which he received the Diamonds), surmounted and surrounded by his initials and the award ribbon, plus two rows of 15 individual bars. Graf would claim ten USAAF four-engined bombers destroyed in Defence of the Reich operations with JG(r) 50, before heading back East to his old unit, JG 52.

GLOSTER GLADIATOR

The ultimate (and final) British biplane fighter of them all, the Gladiator started life as a company private venture. Having produced a vast quantity of Gauntlets in the early 1930s to the previous Spec. F.9/26, Gloster based its new SS.37 very much on this fighter, although by redesigning the wings as single bay units and 'cleaning up' the undercarriage to include internally sprung assemblies, it achieved a top speed of 253mph with the aircraft. The SS.37 boasted four guns as specified by the RAF, but the fighter still embraced the 'old' technology of doped fabric over its wood and metal ribbed and stringered fuselage and wings.

However, with high-performance monoplane bombers in the development stage, the RAF was left with little choice but to accept the Gloster design as an interim machine to tide Fighter Command over until the proposed Hawker and Supermarine designs reached fruition later in the decade – Spec. F.14/35 was quickly written around the SS.37, and a production order placed. Following its first flight in September 1934, the prototype had an enclosed cockpit fitted and a Mercury IX engine of 840hp 'plumbed in' in place of the 645hp Mercury VIS. Following these modifications, the Mk I was put into production, and Gloster built 231 Gladiators. The fighter made its service debut with Nos 3 and 72 Sqns in January 1937, and went on to serve with a further 26 fighter units.

The later Mk II was fitted with the Mercury VIIIA engine of a similar horsepower, although this powerplant boasted automatic mixture control, an electric starter and a Vokes air filter for service in the desert – 252 new-build Mk IIs were delivered, and a number of Mk Is upgraded. Sixty arrestor-hooked Sea Gladiators were also delivered to the Royal Navy, plus a further 165 Mk I/IIs for foreign customers. A considerable number of Gladiators were still in service when war broke out in September 1939, and although virtually obsolete, they gave a good account of themselves in France, North and East Africa and the Mediterranean.

Gladiator II L8009 of Flg Off P. Wykeham-Barnes,
No 80 Sqn, Sidi Barrani, Egypt, August 1940

SPECIFICATIONS
(GLADIATOR I)

Crew: Pilot

Length: 27ft 5in (8.36m)

Wingspan: 32ft 3in (9.83m)

Height: 10ft 4in (3.15m)

Empty: 3,450lb (1,565kg)

Max T/O: 4,750lb (2,155kg)

Max Speed: 253mph (407km/h)

Range: 428 miles (689km)

Powerplant: Bristol Mercury IX

Output: 840hp (626kW)

Armament: Two 0.303in machine guns in nose and two under lower wings

First Flight Date: 12 September 1934 (SS.37)

PLANE DETAILS

Previous page: One of 28 Gladiator IIs built by Gloster in the summer of 1938, this aircraft served with No 80 Sqn in Egypt pre-war, prior to briefly being used by No 3 Sqn Royal Australian Air Force in 1940. Passed back to No 80 Sqn, L8009 claimed the unit's first kills of World War II when future ace Flg Off Peter Wykeham-Barnes shot down an Italian Breda Ba.65 on 4 August 1940. Minutes later the Gladiator was hit by fire from an escorting Fiat CR.42, forcing Wykeham-Barnes to take to his parachute.

Sea Gladiator II N2272 of Sub Lt 'Jimmy' Sleigh, 804 NAS, Hatston, Orkney, July 1940

This page: Fitted with an arrestor hook mid fuselage, N2272 was delivered new to the Fleet Air Arm's 769 Naval Air Squadron (NAS) in May 1939. By June of the following year it was serving with newly formed 804 NAS, which was charged with defending the naval base at Scapa Flow from German bombers. Shore-based at Hatston, 804 NAS also embarked its Sea Gladiators aboard HMS *Glorious* (once) and HMS *Furious* (four times) in 1940, seeing action from the latter carrier over Norway in May.

HAWKER HURRICANE

The Hurricane's arrival in December 1937 saw the RAF make the jump from biplane to monoplane fighters. The aircraft owed much to Hawker's ultimate biplane design, the Fury, both types being built around an internal 'skeleton' of four wire-braced alloy and steel tube longerons. The Hurricane also benefited from Hawker's long-standing partnership with Rolls-Royce, whose Merlin I proved to be the ideal powerplant. Toting eight 0.303in machine guns and capable of speeds in excess of 300mph, the Hurricane I was the world's most advanced fighter when issued to the RAF.

Technically eclipsed by the Spitfire by mid-1940, Hurricanes nevertheless outnumbered the former during the Battle of Britain by three to one, and downed more Luftwaffe aircraft. Even prior to its 'finest hour', Hurricanes provided the first RAF aces of the war in France during the *Blitzkrieg*. In 1940–41 the Mk I saw action in the Mediterranean and North Africa. Finally, in 1942, tropicalised Hurricane Is attempted to halt the Japanese invasion of the Far East, the fighter seeing action over Singapore, Malaya, Burma and Java.

On 11 June 1940 a Hurricane I was flown with a two-stage supercharged Merlin XX engine. Designated the Hurricane Mk II, deliveries of the machine to frontline units commenced in September. Boasting fuselage strengthening to allow the fitment of wings featuring universal attachment points for external stores, the 12-gun Mk IIB was produced from late 1940, and in 1941 the four 20mm cannon Mk IIC made its service debut. All Mk IIs had underwing attachments for bombs, rockets and drop tanks. Although deemed obsolete for the day fighter role in the UK, the Hurricane II served as a fighter-bomber and night intruder on the Channel Coast into 1943. In other theatres, the Hurricane was the most modern fighter available to the Allies. In its Sea Hurricane guise it was also the primary carrier-based fighter in service with the Fleet Air Arm in 1941–42. Although Hurricane production ceased in September 1944, the aircraft remained in frontline service in the Far East until VJ Day.

Hurricane I P2921 of Flt Lt 'Pete' Brothers, No 32 Sqn,
Biggin Hill/Hawkinge, Kent, July 1940

SPECIFICATIONS
(HURRICANE I)

Crew: Pilot

Length: 31ft 5in (9.58m)

Wingspan: 40ft (12.19m)

Height: 13ft (3.96m)

Empty: 4,982lb (2,260kg)

Max T/0: 7,490lb (3,397kg)

Max Speed: 324mph (521km/h)

Range: 600 miles (965km)

Powerplant: Rolls-Royce Merlin II/III

Output: 1,030hp (768kW)

Armament: Eight 0.303in machine guns in wings

First Flight Date: 6 November 1935

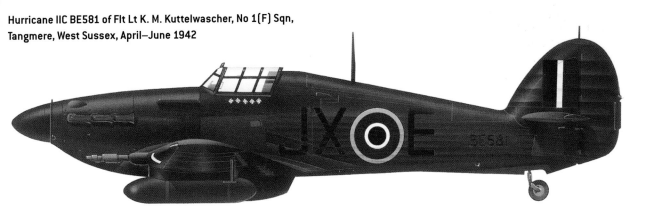

Hurricane IIC BE581 of Flt Lt K. M. Kuttelwascher, No 1(F) Sqn, Tangmere, West Sussex, April–June 1942

PLANE DETAILS

Previous page: This Hurricane was one of three Hawker fighters sent to No 32 Sqn on 11 June 1940 as attrition replacements. As the newest of the three to arrive at Biggin Hill, P2921 was immediately 'acquired' by 'B' Flight commander, 'Pete' Brothers. He flew P2921 throughout July and August 1940, during which time he was credited with destroying eight German aircraft. The fighter remained with No 32 Sqn until 21 February 1941, when it was transferred to newly formed No 315 'Polish' Sqn.

This page: This aircraft was issued new to No 1(F) Sqn in late 1941, and it eventually became leading night intruder ace Karel Kuttelwascher's mount. The Czech pilot downed 15 German bombers near their French bases in this aircraft between 1 April and 1 July 1942. It later served with Nos 486, 253 and 532 Sqns until written off in a night landing accident with the latter unit on 7 November 1942.

JUNKERS Ju 87

One of the most feared weapons of the early war years, the Junker Ju 87 struck terror into the hearts of those unfortunate enough to be on the ground beneath it. Dubbed the Stuka (an abbreviation of *Stürzkampfflugzeug* – dive-bomber aircraft), the prototype had first flown in late 1935 powered by a Rolls-Royce Kestrel engine and fitted with twin fins. By the time it entered series production two years later, the Ju 87B had a solitary fin, a Junkers Jumo 211Da engine and large trousered landing gear. It was every inch a dive-bomber, featuring a heavy bomb crutch that swung the weapon clear of the fuselage before it was released. Capable of diving at angles of up to 80 degrees, the aircraft could deliver more than 1,500lb of ordnance with great accuracy.

First blooded in Spain by the *Condor Legion* in 1937, the Ju 87's finest hour came in support of the *Blitzkrieg* campaign waged by the Wehrmacht in Poland in September 1939 and across Western Europe in May–June 1940. Its moderate speed in level flight and general lack of manoeuvrability were quickly exposed during the Battle of Britain, however, making the Stuka highly vulnerable to RAF fighters. Licking their wounds, the *Stukageschwader* were sent south-east from France to the warmer climes of the Balkans and the Mediterranean, where, due to a paucity of Allied fighters, the effectiveness of the Ju 87 as a precision weapon of war returned. The aircraft duly took a heavy toll on troops and ships. This continued in North Africa, where the B-model Stukas were supplanted by the faster Ju 87D, powered by the 1,400hp Jumo 211J engine.

From June 1941 the Stuka also became a familiar sight in the war-torn skies of Eastern Europe, as it once again spearheaded the *Blitzkrieg* campaign against the USSR. Here, the 37mm cannon-equipped Ju 87G tank buster also saw much action against Soviet mechanised divisions. By the autumn of 1943 surviving Stukas (of the 5,709 examples built) had been relegated to operating under the cover of darkness on all fronts due to their vulnerability to Allied fighters in daylight hours.

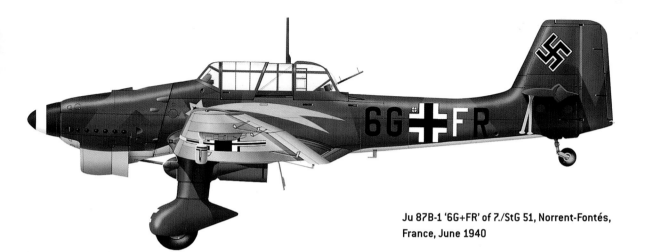

Ju 87B-1 '6G+FR' of 7./StG 51, Norrent-Fontés,
France, June 1940

SPECIFICATIONS (Ju 87D)

Crew: Pilot and rear gunner

Length: 37ft 8.75in (11.50m)

Wingspan: 45ft 3.25in (13.80m)

Height: 12ft 9.25in (3.90m)

Empty: 8,600lb (3,900kg)

Max T/O: 14,550lb (6,600kg)

Max Speed: 255mph (410km/h)

Range: 954 miles (1,535km)

Powerplant: Junkers Jumo 211J-1

Output: 1,400hp (1,044kW)

Armament: Two fixed MG 17 7.92mm machine
guns in wings and one MG 15 7.92mm machine
gun on flexible mounting in rear cockpit;
maximum bomb load of 3,968lb (1,800kg) on
centreline and various gun/bomb options up to
1,102lb (500kg) on underwing racks

First Flight Date: Late 1935

Ju 87D 'S7+CL' of 3./StG 3, Gambut, Libya, November 1942

PLANE DETAILS

Previous page: Perhaps the most flamboyant of all Stuka unit emblems during the early war years, 7./StG 51's badge combined a charging bull on a yellow star background beneath the windscreen, with a yellow comet trail stretching back almost the entire length of the cockpit canopy. III./StG 51 saw much action in the Low Countries and the early phase of the Battle of Britain, before being redesignated II./StG 1 in early July 1940.

This page: One of the first Ju 87Ds to reach North Africa, this aircraft saw service with 3./StG 3 during the pivotal battle of El Alamein. Fitted with the more powerful Jumo 211J engine, the *Dora* differed externally from earlier models of Stuka in featuring a 'cleaned up' nose and canopy design, which included moving the engine coolant radiators to under the wings.

SUPERMARINE SPITFIRE

The Spitfire was the only British fighter to remain in production throughout World War II – more than 22,500 were produced in mark numbers ranging from I through to 24 – and its exploits are legendary. Designed by R. J. Mitchell following his experiences with the RAF's Schneider Trophy winning Supermarine seaplanes of the 1920s and 30s, prototype Spitfire K5054 first took to the skies on 5 March 1936, powered by the famous Rolls-Royce Merlin I engine. However, due to production problems encountered with the fighter's revolutionary stressed-skin construction, it was to be another 2½ years before the first Spitfires entered service.

During its nine-year production life, the Spitfire's shape was to alter very little, but under the skin the story was very different. The power output of the Merlin was increased to allow the fighter to compete on level terms with new German types, with firstly the Mk V and then the Mk IX proving to be a match for the Bf 109F/G and Fw 190 at virtually all altitudes. The Spitfire also performed sterling service in the photo-reconnaissance and fighter-bomber roles, as well as being modified into a carrier fighter for the Fleet Air Arm, which called its aircraft the Seafire.

From late 1942, Rolls-Royce Griffon-powered Spitfires were amongst the most impressive piston-engined fighters of their time. The Spitfire Mk XIV in particular was an awesome fighter to fly thanks to the generous levels of horsepower cranked out by its Griffon engine, which more than offset the mark's increased weight due to the strengthening of the fuselage in preparation for the fitment of the new powerplant. Only 957 production Mk XIVs were built, with the type's finest hour coming in mid 1944 when its straight-line speed was used to counter the V1 menace during air defence patrols over south-east England – the Spitfire XIV could outpace all other Allied piston-engined fighter types. The photo-reconnaissance PR XIX also saw service in the final weeks of the war as the first of 225 examples arrived in the frontline. Griffon Spitfires served with the RAF until the late 1950s.

Spitfire Mk IB R6776 of Flt Sgt G. Unwin, No 19 Sqn,
Fowlmere, Cambridgeshire, August/September 1940

SPECIFICATIONS
(SPITFIRE IX)

Crew: Pilot

Length: 31ft 1in (9.47m)

Wingspan: 36ft 10in (11.23m)

Height: 12ft 7.75in (3.86m)

Empty: 6,200lb (2,812kg)

Max T/O: 9,500lb (4,309kg)

Max Speed: 408mph (657km/h)

Range: 434 miles (698km)

Powerplant: Rolls-Royce Merlin 61

Output: 1,565hp (1,167kW)

Armament: Two Hispano 20mm cannon and four Browning 0.303in machine guns in wings; maximum bomb load of 1,000lb (454kg) on underwing racks

First Flight Date: 5 March 1936

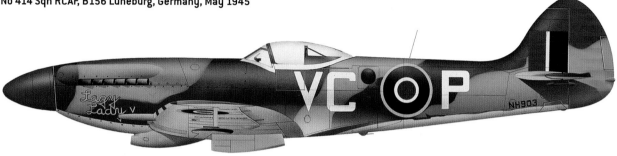

Spitfire FR XIV NH903 of Sqn Ldr J. B. Prendergast,
No 414 Sqn RCAF, B156 Luneburg, Germany, May 1945

PLANE DETAILS

Previous page: This aircraft was one of the original cannon-armed Spitfire IBs issued to No 19 Sqn for a brief period in the summer of 1940. High-scoring ace George Unwin enjoyed success in R6776, claiming a Bf 110 destroyed and another probably destroyed on 16 August, followed by a third Bf 110 confirmed destroyed on 3 September. Later, the aircraft was modified into a Mk VB and served with Nos 92, 316 and 306 Sqns, before being written off in May 1942 after sustaining battle damage over France.

This page: In early 1945 the Spitfire XIV began being used by some 2nd Tactical Air Force (TAF) fighter reconnaissance units, including No 414 Sqn. On 2 May unit CO Sqn Ldt Jim Prendergast shot down two Fw 190s over Weismar harbour in this aircraft during an armed reconnaissance. Prendergast's personal mount acquired attractive nose art post-war, and it remained with the RAF as part of the occupation forces until written off in a landing accident at Wunstorf while serving with No 2 Sqn on 19 May 1950.

SHORT SUNDERLAND

A military development of the majestic Imperial Airways C-Class 'Empire' flying boats of the 1930s, the Sunderland was the RAF's principal maritime patrol aircraft of World War II. Flown in prototype form for the first time on 16 October 1937, production examples started entering frontline service with No 230 Sqn in Singapore and No 210 Sqn in the UK in the summer of 1938. Established within Coastal Command ranks by the outbreak of World War II, the Sunderland was soon providing convoy escort and anti-submarine cover in the Atlantic, Middle and Far East and the Mediterranean.

Although seemingly vulnerable to aerial attack, the Sunderland proved difficult to shoot down thanks to its numerous 0.303in machine guns – as many as 12 could be fitted in three turrets and various hatches, earning the aircraft the nickname the 'Flying Porcupine'.

A total of 749 Sunderlands were built (by Shorts and Blackburn) in four distinctive marks, featuring ever more powerful radial engines, varying degrees of protective armament, extra fuel capacity and modified hull shapes. The Mk III, with additional fuel capacity and gun armament, a redesigned main step on the planing hull and, crucially, air-surface vessel radar, was the most produced – some 462 examples were issued to RAF, RCAF, RNZAF and RAAF units from December 1941.

By the end of the war, no less than 28 RAF squadrons were flying Sunderlands. The last example (a Mk V fitted with more powerful and reliable Twin Wasp engines) was built by Shorts in June 1946, and the aircraft remained in service with RAF Coastal Command and the RNZAF until 1959.

During its 14 years of post-war service the Sunderland MR 5 was used in the Berlin Airlift, the Korean War, in Malaya against communist terrorists and on the North Greenland Expedition. Many surplus Sunderlands were stripped of their armament and fitted out as airliners post-war, these flying boats being christened Sandringhams.

Sunderland III W3981 of No 201 Sqn, Castle Archdale,
Northern Ireland, October 1941

SPECIFICATIONS
(SUNDERLAND III)

Crew: Pilot and co-pilot, flight engineer, radio
operator, radar operator, navigator and bow,
dorsal, tail and beam gunners

Length: 85ft 4in (26.01m)

Wingspan: 112ft 9.50in (34.38m)

Height: 32ft 10.50in (10.02m)

Empty: 34,500lb (15,663kg)

Max T/O: 58,000lb (26,308kg)

Max Speed: 210mph (338km/h)

Range: 2,900 miles (4,670km)

Powerplant: four Bristol Pegasus XVIIIs

Output: 4,260hp (2,382kW)

Armament: Two Browning 0.303in machine guns
in nose and dorsal turrets and four in tail turret,
plus two-four additional guns in nose and upper
beam positions; maximum bomb/mine/depth
charge load of 2,000lb (907kg) on underwing
racks

First Flight Date: 16 October 1937

Sunderland GR V RN282 of No 461 Sqn, Pembroke Dock, Wales, May 1945

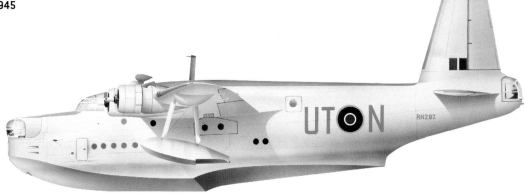

PLANE DETAILS

Previous page: With its camouflaged uppersurfaces and very low demarcation between the topside colours and the undersides, W3981's appearance was typical of early war Sunderlands. Built by Shorts in Rochester during the summer of 1941, this aircraft initially served with No 204 Sqn prior to being transferred to No 201 Sqn. Passed on to No 4 (Coastal) OTU, W3981 served in Training Command for more than two years before it was struck off charge on 1 July 1944.

This page: One of 30 Mk Vs built by Blackburn in Dumbarton, this aircraft was delivered new to No 461 Sqn RAAF at Pembroke Dock in early 1945. This particular Sunderland was one of the first to feature the predominantly white colour scheme that was subsequently commonplace on post-war RAF flying boats. RN282 was finally struck off charge on 13 May 1958, having flown with Nos 10 RAAF, 201, 88, 209 and 205 Sqns during a frontline career that lasted 13 years.

MESSERSCHMITT Bf 110

Designed in 1934–35 to fill the perceived need for a high-speed, long-range, heavily-armed twin-engined fighter, Messerschmitt's Bf 110 *Zerstörer* (destroyer) fulfilled all these criterion. Seen as the ultimate bomber escort, capable of sweeping the skies clean of enemy fighters, the Bf 110 relied more on its firepower than manoeuvrability to survive in combat. Too late to see action in the Spanish Civil War, the Daimler-Benz DB 601-powered Bf 110C made the aircraft's combat debut over Poland, where it dominated the skies in an environment of overwhelming Luftwaffe air superiority. These successes continued throughout the 'Phoney War' and into the early days of the *Blitzkrieg* in the West, but come the Battle of Britain serious flaws in the *Zerstörer* concept were graphically exposed. The large twin-engined machine, although powerfully armed, was simply no match for the more agile Spitfire and Hurricane. As if to prove this point, in the latter stages of the Battle of Britain Bf 109s were having to escort the fighter escorts!

Following the loss of more than 200 Bf 110s during the campaign, the day fighter role was given over almost exclusively to the single-seat *gruppe*, and the Messerschmitt 'twin' sent further afield to operate either on less hostile fronts like the Balkans, the Mediterranean and North Africa, or in the rapidly developing nightfighter role.

The latter mission was ideally suited to a big fighter like the Bf 110, and by 1943, the dedicated, radar-equipped, G-model accounted for around 60 per cent of the overall *Nachtjagd* force. The most effective nightfighter variant was the G-4, which boasted more powerful DB 605B-1 engines, FuG 212 Lichtenstein C-1, SN-2 or 221a radar and various cannon fits, depending on the sub-type. The Bf 110G-4 was also the mount of choice for leading nightfighter aces Heinz-Wolfgang Schnaufer (121 victories) and Helmut Lent (102 victories). So effective was the Bf 110G in this nocturnal role that the fighter remained in production until March 1945, by which time 6,050 *Zerstörer* had been built.

Bf 110G-4 'G9+EZ' of Oberleutnant Heinz-Wolfgang Schnaufer, *Staffelkapitän* of 12./NJG 1, St Trond, Belgium, February 1944

SPECIFICATIONS
(Bf 110C-4)

Crew: Pilot and radio operator/gunner

Length: 39ft 8.5in (12.10m)

Wingspan: 53ft 4.75in (16.27m)

Height: 11ft 6in (3.50m)

Empty: 9,920lb (4,500kg)

Max T/O: 15,300lb (6,940kg)

Max Speed: 349mph (561km/h)

Range: 565 miles (909km)

Powerplants: two Daimler-Benz DB 601A-1 engines

Output: 2,200hp (1,640kW)

Armament: Two 20mm cannon and four 7.9mm machine guns in nose cowling, 7.9mm machine gun in rear cockpit

First Flight Date: 12 May 1936

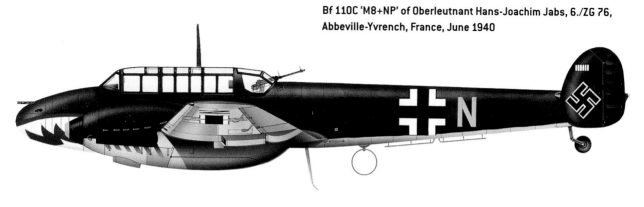

Bf 110C 'M8+NP' of Oberleutnant Hans-Joachim Jabs, 6./ZG 76, Abbeville-Yvrench, France, June 1940

PLANE DETAILS

Previous page: Oberleutnant Schnaufer enjoyed success with this Bf 110G-4, fitted with FuG 202 radar, flame damper shrouds, an extended barrel nose cannon and *Schräge Musik*, on at least five occasions in 1943–44. The aircraft wears typical nightfighter markings for the period, the *Nachtjagd* making less use of colour in regard to *Staffel* letters and so forth than other branches of the Luftwaffe. Its rudder bears a tally of 47 kills scored by Schnaufer up to that time, his most recent being on the night of 14 February 1944.

This page: Wearing standard early war camouflage (schwarzgrün 70/dunkelgrün 71 uppersurfaces and hellblau 65 undersides) and a textbook set of national insignia of the period, this aircraft also boasts the most famous Bf 110 unit marking of them all – II./ZG 76's distinctive 'sharksmouth'. Representative of the *gruppe* at the height of its power, Jabs' machine is depicted during ZG 76's headlong advance across France in the late spring/early summer of 1940. His first six kills are already displayed on the tailfin of the big 'fighter-destroyer'.

FIAT CR.42 FALCO

The last Fiat biplane fighter (and effectively the last of its type in the world), the Falco, like its stylish predecessor the CR.32, was obsolete before the outbreak of World War II. Despite this, great numbers saw action during the conflict not only with the Italians, but also the Finns, Germans, Hungarians and Belgians.

A development of the unsuccessful CR.41, the CR.42 was created by legendary Fiat biplane designer Celestino Rosatelli. Extremely light on the controls, well liked by those that flew it and superbly agile, the Falco was the ultimate biplane fighter. However, it had the misfortune to be conceived at a time when the biplane had already been eclipsed by the monoplane as the universal fighter configuration. The prototype made its first flight as late as 23 May 1938, by which point the CR.42 was already conceptually obsolete. Nevertheless, the first examples entered frontline service with the *Regia Aeronautica* in April 1939, followed by a handful of other export countries, including neutral Sweden. Production continued through to 1943, by which time 1,781 CR.42s had been constructed in four main variants that covered day fighter, nightfighter and close support roles.

The Falco saw considerable action in the Belgian, Greek, East African, Western European, Mediterranean and North African theatres. Indeed, it was the *Regia Aeronautica's* staple fighter in both North and East Africa, Greece and over Malta in 1940–41, during which time its pilots routinely fought with British and Commonwealth squadrons equipped in the main with Hurricanes and Gladiators. A number of Italian pilots claimed their first victories with the Falco, including Mario Visintini, who was the most successful biplane ace of World War II. As the Fiat fighter became more and more vulnerable in its designed role, however, survivors were relegated to performing nocturnal patrols over northern Italy. Small numbers of CR.42s remained in service with the Luftwaffe as night ground attack platforms in the Balkans and northern Italy following the Italian surrender in September 1943.

CR.42CN Falco of Capitano L. Marcolin, CO of 377ª *Squadriglia Autonoma*, Palermo-Boccadifalco, Sicily, autumn 1942

SPECIFICATIONS
(CR.42 FALCO)

Crew: Pilot

Length: 27ft 3in (8.30m)

Wingspan: 31ft 10in (9.70m)

Height: 10ft 10in (3.30m)

Empty: 3,763lb (1,707kg)

Max T/O: 5,302lb (2,405kg)

Max Speed: 266mph (428km/h)

Range: 481 miles (775km)

Powerplant: Fiat A 74 RC38

Output: 840hp (626kW)

Armament: Two 12.7mm machine guns in nose

First Flight Date: 23 May 1938

PLANE DETAILS

Previous page:
Tasked with defending the night skies of Sicily, 377ª *Squadriglia* was based at Palermo-Boccadifalco in 1942–43. A section of CR.42CNs was attached to the unit in September 1942 for nightfighter and anti-submarine duties. The squadron CO during this period was Luciano Marcolin, who had also seen action in the Spanish Civil War. The unit's specialised mission is well reflected in its choice of unit emblem.

This page: Mario Visintini was the top-scoring biplane ace of World War II. A veteran of the Spanish Civil War, where he

CR.42 Falco (serial unknown) of Tenente Mario Visintini, 412ª *Squadriglia Autonoma*, Barentu, Eritrea, late 1940

claimed one victory in the CR.32, he was officially credited with 16 and two shared kills with the CR.42 in East Africa prior to his death in a flying accident on 11 February 1941. Camouflaged in the standard Italian three-tone scheme of the period, this aircraft lacks specific East African theatre markings apart from the 412ª *Squadriglia* unit emblem of a red prancing horse over a black silhouette of Africa.

JUNKERS Ju 88

One of the Luftwaffe's most important, and versatile, combat aircraft types, the Ju 88 was developed to answer a requirement for a high-speed medium bomber with a dive-bombing capability. First flown in prototype form in December 1936, production A-1s entered service in September 1939. Boasting a formidable bomb load and good performance, the Ju 88 proved less vulnerable to enemy fighters than its contemporaries the Heinkel He 111 and Dornier Do 17 thanks to the aircraft's more modern design and better engines.

Continually upgraded and reworked during World War II, around 2,000 Ju 88 bombers were built each year between 1940–43 – close to 15,000 Ju 88s had been delivered by the war's end. Junkers also split off the Ju 188 and 388 bomber families from the parent Ju 88, allowing it to then concentrate on the high-performance S-series.

Although designed first and foremost for the fast medium bomber role, the Ju 88 was easily modified into a *Zerstörer* heavy fighter, and the first such aircraft flew as early as 1939. The primary changes carried out to the basic A-model airframe centred on the replacement of the former's glazed nose with a solid fairing (equipped with both cannon and machine guns) and modification of the aircraft's bomb-bay to house a weapons gondola. The evolution of the C-model heavy fighter mirrored that of the Ju 88 bomber, with more powerful engines, greater span wings and a strengthened fuselage being incorporated into the *Zerstörer*.

A small number of Ju 88Cs made the type's combat debut over Poland in September 1939, and from then on heavy fighter variants saw action on every front up to VE-Day. The ultimate fighter version was the Ju 88G of 1944, which boasted a FuG 220 or 227 radar, cannon and machine gun armament and advanced Junkers Jumo or BMW engines. A dedicated nightfighter, the first Ju 88G-1s entered service with the *Nachtjagd* in mid-1944, and they remained a potent threat to Bomber Command through to May 1945.

Ju 88S-1 'Z6-BH' of 1./KG 66, Avord, France, April 1944

SPECIFICATIONS
(Ju 88A-1)

Crew: Pilot, navigator, bomb aimer/gunner and two/three ventral/dorsal gunners

Length: 36ft 5in (11.10m)

Wingspan: 65ft 10.50in (20.08m)

Height: 15ft 11in (4.85m)

Empty: 21,737lb (9,860kg)

Max T/O: 30,865lb (14,000kg)

Max Speed: 292mph (470km/h)

Range: 1,696 miles (2,730km)

Powerplant: two Junkers Jumo 211Fs

Output: 2,680hp (2,000kW)

Armament: One MG 17 7.92mm machine gun in cockpit, one/two on flexible mounting in nose, two in rear cockpit and one/two in ventral gondola; maximum bomb load of 4,409lb (2,000kg) in bomb-bay and on underwing racks

First Flight Date: 21 December 1936

Ju 88A-5 'F1+BD' of *Stab* **III./KG 76, Illesheim, Germany, February 1941**

PLANE DETAILS

Previous page: The pathfinder Ju 88s of I./KG 66 were heavily engaged in the *Steinbock* offensive against England in early 1944, its aircraft being night-camouflaged in a dense dapple of dark grey spots over all blue-grey uppersurfaces. The bomber's national insignia was still prominent, but its four-digit code 'Z6-BH' was almost lost high up on the tailfin to the right of the swastika.

This page: III./KG 76 was one of the last *Kampfgruppen* to convert from the He 111 to the Ju 88 and see brief action in the Blitz on England prior to joining the mass exodus of Luftwaffe units to Poland in preparation for the invasion of the USSR in June 1941. The bomber is wearing a textbook finish and markings for this period, this *Stabskette* machine sporting tricolour spinners representing all three subordinate *Staffeln* within III./KG 76.

MITSUBISHI A6M ZERO-SEN

The A6M was developed by Mitsubishi to meet a demanding Imperial Japanese Navy (IJN) requirement for a replacement to the successful A5M of the late 1930s. Officially designated the Navy Type O Carrier Fighter Rei-sen ('Zero Fighter'), the A6M offered an impressive mix of high performance, long range and superb manoeuvrability in a lightweight and modestly powered airframe. Prototype A6M1s were powered by the Mitsubishi Zuisei 13, and a switch was soon made to the Sakae, which was retained until war's end.

Redesignated the A6M2, the first production-standard Model 11s were delivered to the IJN in July 1940. Two months later production switched to the Model 21, this variant having folding wingtips for deck elevator compatibility. A6M2s made up two-thirds of the IJN's fighter force by 7 December 1941, and 135 Zeros took part in the Pearl Harbor assault. By then the re-engined A6M3 was just entering production, the new variant being powered by a supercharged Sakae 21 rated at 1,130hp (843kW).

The most produced of all Zero variants, the A6M5, was initially developed by Mitsubishi as a 'stop gap' fighter until the A7M Reppu was cleared for production. However, terminal delays with the later resulted in the A6M5 remaining in production until war's end. Retaining the airframe, powerplant and armament of the A6M3, the 'new' Zero was fitted with modified flaps and ailerons and thickened wing skinning to allow pilots to attain greater terminal speeds whilst attempting to dive away from Allied fighters. The A6M5 reached the frontline in October 1943, and by March 1944 the first sub-variants were rolling off the production line. Thoroughly outclassed by the US Navy and USAAF fighters in-theatre, hundreds of A6M5s were lost during the Pacific battles of 1944–45. In an attempt to redress the balance, Mitsubishi mated a water/methanol-injected Sakai 31 with an A6M5 Model 52c to produce the A6M7 Model 63. Limited production commenced in May 1945, but only 150 had been completed by VJ Day.

A6M2 Model 21 of PO2/c Yoshiro Hashiguchi,
3rd Kokutai, Surabaya, Java, February 1942

SPECIFICATIONS
(A6M2 MODEL 21)

Crew: Pilot

Length: 29ft 8.75in (9.06m)

Wingspan: 39ft 4.25in (12m)

Height: 10ft 0.15in (3.05m)

Empty: 3,704lb (1,680kg)

Max T/O: 6,164lb (2,796kg)

Max Speed: 331mph (533km/h)

Range: 1,162 miles (1,870km)

Powerplant: Nakajima NK1C Sakae 12

Output: 950hp (708kW)

Armament: Two 7.7mm machine guns in nose and
two 20mm cannon in wings; provision for two
underwing 132lb (60kg) bombs

First Flight Date: 1 April 1939

A6M5 Model 52 of CPO Takeo Tanimizu, 203rd Kokutai, Kasan-bara, Japan, June 1945

PLANE DETAILS

Previous page: Various pilots flew this particular aircraft in 1941–42, adding their victories to the tally on the fighter's fin. However, most of these successes were claimed by PO2/c Yoshiro Hashiguchi, who subsequently saw action in the Solomons and the Philippines. An ace with more than ten victories to his name, Hashiguchi perished on 25 October 1944 when he went down with the light aircraft carrier *Chiyoda* after it was shelled by the American heavy cruiser USS *Wisconsin* during the battle of Cape Engaño.

This page: The unusual kill markings on this aircraft consist of two head-on silhouettes of B-29s, which represent one probable and another that Tanimizu jointly shot down with high-scoring ace CPO Tetsu Iwamoto. The five stars with arrows indicate confirmed kills, whilst the single unpierced star denotes a probable or damaged claim. Tanimizu survived the war with 18 victories to his name, whilst the battered hulk of his Zero-sen was photographed in a Nagasaki hangar in November 1945.

CURTISS P-40 WARHAWK

Overshadowed by other more successful USAAF fighter types like the P-38 Lightning, P-47 Thunderbolt and P-51 Mustang, the Curtiss P-40 was nevertheless the primary USAAF fighter at the time of the Japanese fleet's surprise attack on Pearl Harbor on 7 December 1941. The Warhawk was subsequently responsible for 'holding the line' in the Pacific for much of 1942, vainly attempting to blunt the aerial onslaught unleashed by the Japanese.

The last in a long line of fighters to carry the appellation 'Hawk', the P-40 family was born out of the marriage of an early-production Curtiss P-36A fuselage with the all-new Allison V-1710-19 liquid-cooled inline engine. When first flown as the Hawk 81, Curtiss engineers could never have imagined that roughly 13,800 aircraft would be built between early 1939 and December 1944, and used in virtually every theatre of conflict during World War II.

Although the Allison engine was initially the P-40's strong point, it soon became its Achilles' heel, as it quickly 'ran out of steam' above 15,000ft due to it lacking a turbo or supercharger. This made the Warhawk inferior to virtually all other Axis fighters above certain ceilings, and reduced it to a life of ground attack work, where its durability and crisp handling made it a favourite with Allied pilots.

Nevertheless, the fighter saw widespread combat in every theatre during World War II from the deserts of North Africa to the frozen tundra of Arctic Russia. Perhaps the most famous of all P-40s to see action were the 100+ Model 81-A-2 Tomahawks issued to the American Volunteer Group (dubbed the 'Flying Tigers' thanks to the 'sharksmouths' that adorned the aircraft) in China and Burma in late 1941. The aircraft was also widely used by the USAAF in the Pacific, China and the Mediterranean, where obsolescent Warhawks saw widespread service as fighter-bombers supporting Allied troops engaging the enemy at close quarters through to the war's end.

Hawk 81-A-2 number '75' (CAF serial P-8186) of Third Sqn
Flt Ldr W. Reed, Kunming, China, January 1942

SPECIFICATIONS (P-40B)

Crew: Pilot

Length: 31ft 8.5in (9.66m)

Wingspan: 37ft 3.5in (11.37m)

Height: 10ft 7in (3.22m)

Empty: 5,812lb (2,636kg)

Max T/O: 8,058lb (3,655kg)

Max Speed: 345mph (555km/h)

Range: 800 miles (1,287km)

Powerplant: Allison V-1710-33

Output: 1,040hp (775kW)

Armament: Two 0.50in machine guns in nose and two or four 0.30in machine guns in wings

First Flight Date: 14 October 1938

P-40F-1 41-14081 'White 43' of Capt R. E. 'Deke' Whittaker, 65th FS/57th FG, Hani Main, Tunisia, April–May 1943

PLANE DETAILS

Previous page: Bill Reed will forever be remembered as the 'assigned' pilot of this Tomahawk. The ultimate fate of the aeroplane is not yet certain, but it is likely that the fighter was lost on 10 March 1942 when Reed and four others were forced to crash-land after they ran out of fuel near Loiwing. Like all AVG pilots, Reed actually flew many different aircraft on operations, including Tomahawk 69 (P-8115), Tomahawk 79 (P-8135), Tomahawk 74 (P-8193) and Tomahawk 59 (P-8161), to name but four.

This page: Roy Whittaker, top ace of the 57th FG, flew two similarly marked Warhawks during his combat tour, and this was the second of them. The aeroplane features Whittaker's full score of seven victories, and it also displays the 65th FS 'Fighting Cocks' badge on the nose. Note that swastikas have been used to mark all of Whittaker's kills, although two of his victims were Italian aircraft. 41-14081 was lost in October 1943, several months after Whittaker had completed his combat tour.

NORTH AMERICAN B-25 MITCHELL

North American's response to a pre-war USAAC request for a twin-engined medium bomber, the B-25 Mitchell, proved to be one of the most venerable, and versatile, combat aircraft to see action in World War II. Tailored to fit USAAC Circular Proposal 38-385, the NA-40 prototype carried out successful flight trials, but North American was encouraged to further improve its design by the army, which now stated that any future medium bomber would have to carry a payload of 2,400lb – twice that originally stipulated in 38-385. Re-engineered and considerably enlarged, the definitive production airframe was designated the NA-62. So impressed with what it saw on the drawing board, the USAAC ordered 184 aircraft (to be designated the B-25) before metal had even been cut on the revised design.

The first production standard machine was flown on 19 August 1940, by which point it had been christened the Mitchell, after maverick army bomber proponent William 'Billy' Mitchell. Like a number of other USAAC types then entering service, the B-25 benefited from the lessons being bitterly learned by the combatants in Europe, and crew armour plating and self-sealing tanks were fitted into production machines by North American – these aircraft were designated B-25As.

Gaining early fame in the Doolittle Raid on Tokyo in April 1942, the Mitchell fought not only with the USAAF in the Pacific, but also with Marine Corps, British, Dutch and Australian units. The Marine Corps designated its Mitchells PBJ-1s, and more than 700 were received between 1943 and 1945. These aircraft equipped eight frontline units within the Marine Medium Bombardment Group, the latter waging war against the Japanese from South Pacific islands in the final 18 months of the conflict. By war's end the Mitchell was still in production, having outlasted its rivals from Douglas and Martin to become the most prolific American medium bomber of World War II – built to the tune of 9,889 airframes. TB-25 pilot/aircrew trainers, based on the prolific B-25J, served with the USAF until 1959.

B-25C Mitchell 41-12480 of Capt R. Lower, 81st BS/12th BG, Bolling Field, Washington, D.C., July 1943

SPECIFICATIONS (B-25J)

Crew: Pilot, co-pilot, bombardier/nose gunner, navigator, dorsal and tail turret gunners

Length: 52ft 11in (16.13m)

Wingspan: 67ft 7in (20.60m)

Height: 16ft 4in (4.98m)

Empty: 19,480lb (8,836kg)

Max T/O: 35,000lb (15,876kg)

Max Speed: 272mph (438km/h)

Range: 1,350 miles (2,173km)

Powerplant: two Wright R-2600-92 Cyclones

Output: 3,400hp (2,535kW)

Armament: Four fixed Browning 0.50in machine guns on fuselage sides, two on flexible mounts in nose, two in dorsal and tail turrets and two in waist; maximum bomb load of 3,000lb (1,361kg) in bomb-bay, plus wing racks for rockets

First Flight Date: January 1939 (NA-40)

PBJ-1D Mitchell 'White 8' (BuNo unknown) of VMB-612,
Saipan and Iwo Jima, spring 1945

PLANE DETAILS

Previous page: Named *DESERT WARRIOR*, 41-12480 completed 73 combat missions from Hergla, Tunisia, before it was selected to represent the medium bomb groups equipped with B-25s in the Mediterranean Theatre of Operations during one of the many US War Bond drives undertaken by armed forces across America. Given a Hollywood-style paint job on its nose, which included a detailed mission log and campaign map, the bomber was manned by seven handpicked crewmen from all four units in the 12th BG during the tour.

This page: This aircraft displays an unusual, but appropriate, method of recording missions by the application of miniature rocket silhouettes. Note the aircraft's prominent AN/APS-3 search radar scanner housed in the nose fairing. This equipment was initially mounted ventrally on earlier PBJ-1s, but the 'hose nose' fairing was preferred by bombardier-navigators as it reduced the level of 'sea clutter' on their radar scopes to a bare minimum.

GRUMMAN F4F WILDCAT

Derived from a biplane design (XF4F-1) offered in competition to the more modern Brewster F2A, the Wildcat was the result of a revised study into the feasibility of a monoplane naval fighter undertaken by Grumman in the summer of 1936. Designated the XF4F-2, the prototype lost out to the rival Brewster in the fly-off due to the latter fighter's superior handling qualities. However, Grumman reworked the design into the vastly superior XF4F-3, fitting a more powerful Pratt & Whitney Twin Wasp engine with a two-stage supercharger, increasing the fighter's wingspan and redesigning its tail surfaces.

France provided Grumman with its first order for the aircraft, committing to 100 G-36As (the export designation for the F4F) in early 1939. Following flight trials, the US Navy also ordered 78 Grumman fighters in August 1939. These began entering service as F4F-3 Wildcats with VF-7 and VF-41 in December 1940, followed by VF-42, VF-71 and Marine Corps squadrons VMF-121, VMF-211 and VMF-221 early the following year. By

then Grumman had switched production to the F4F-4, which incorporated lessons learned from the Royal Navy's combat experience with its ex-French G-36s, which it called Martlet Is – the Fleet Air Arm used various marks from 1940 through to VE Day. The F4F-4 (1,169 built) had its armament boosted from four to six 0.50in guns, self-sealing tanks and wing folding. The Wildcat proved to be a worthy opponent for the Japanese A6M Zero-sen during the battles of Coral Sea and Midway in 1942, as well as the stubborn defence of Guadalcanal.

By 1943 General Motors (GM) had commenced building F4F-4s, which it redesignated FM-1s (839 built). Later that year GM switched production to the FM-2, which utilised a turbocharged Wright R-1820-56 Cyclone in place of the Twin Wasp. This swap made for an improved top speed and an optimum altitude 50 per cent higher than that of the FM-1. By the time production was terminated in August 1945, 4,467 FM-2s had been built. Although replaced in larger fleet 'flat tops' by the F6F Hellcat, the Wildcat served until VJ Day aboard escort carriers.

F4F-4 BuNo 03450/'white 50' of Capt J. Jacob Foss,
VMF-121, Guadalcanal, Solomon Islands,
November 1942

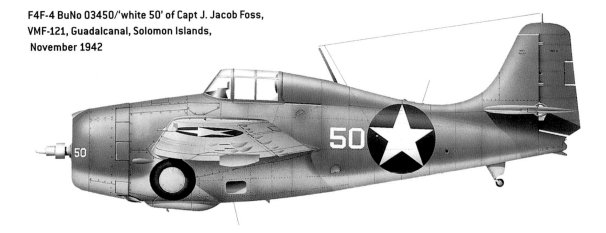

SPECIFICATIONS (F4F-4)

Crew: Pilot

Length: 28ft 9in (8.76m)

Wingspan: 38ft (11.58m)

Height: 11ft 4in (3.45m)

Empty: 5,895lb (2,674kg)

Max T/O: 7,952lb (3,607kg)

Max Speed: 320mph (515km/h)

Range: 770 miles (1,239km)

Powerplant: Pratt & Whitney R-1830-86 Twin Wasp

Output: 1,200hp (895kW)

Armament: Six Browning 0.50in machine guns in wings; maximum bomb load of 200lb (91kg) on underwing racks

First Flight Date: 2 September 1937

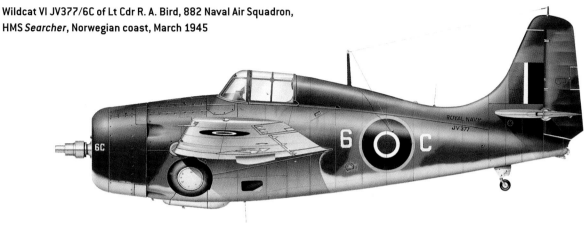

Wildcat VI JV377/6C of Lt Cdr R. A. Bird, 882 Naval Air Squadron, HMS *Searcher*, Norwegian coast, March 1945

PLANE DETAILS

Previous page: This aircraft was used by the Marine Corps' ranking ace, Joe Foss, to down at least one of the 19 Zeros he destroyed during his Guadalcanal tour. BuNo 03450 was entirely representative of 'Cactus Air Force' Wildcats in 1942–43, bearing no personal or unit markings. Foss' logbook reveals that he flew no fewer than 34 different Wildcats during his tour in the Solomon Islands, and claimed kills in ten of them.

This page: Lt Cdr Bird led his unit into action in this aircraft on 26 March 1945 in what proved to be the last productive Fleet Air Arm operation of the war in the Wildcat. He claimed one of four Bf 109Gs from III./JG 5 that were shot down off Tustna Island during a sweep over Norway. Bird also claimed a second Messerschmitt fighter damaged. JV377 features a numeral and letter combination for its code, which was common marking practice amongst Martlet/Wildcat units in World War II.

DOUGLAS SBD DAUNTLESS

The SBD Dauntless was the scourge of the Japanese Imperial Fleet in the crucial years of the Pacific war. Almost single-handedly, 54 SBDs from the US Navy carriers *Enterprise*, *Hornet* and *Yorktown* won the pivotal Battle of Midway on 4 June 1942, destroying four Japanese 'flat tops' in just 24 hours. The SBD of 1942 could trace its origins back to rival designs penned by gifted engineers John Northrop and Ed Heinemann in the mid 1930s. Northrop produced the BT-1 for the US Navy in the spring of 1938, its revolutionary all-metal stressed-skin design exhibiting airframe strength that made it an ideal candidate for adoption as a dive-bomber.

By the time the BT-1 had evolved into the BT-2, with engine and structural changes that made the revised dive-bomber virtually an all-new aircraft, Northrop had become the El Segundo Division of Douglas. The XBT-2 prototype was reworked still further by Heinemann and his team and duly redesignated the SBD-1. Production orders for 57 SBD-1s and 87 SBD-2s were placed by the US Navy in April 1939, with all the 'Dash-1s' going to the Marine Corps in 1940–41. The first unit to receive the Dauntless, as it was now called, was VMB-2 in late 1940, followed by VMB-1 early the following year. The SBD-2s, with extra armament and fuel capacity, had reached US Navy squadrons VB-6 and VS-6 aboard *Enterprise* and VB-2 aboard *Lexington* by the end of 1941.

The definitive SBD-3, and near-identical SBD-4, entered production in the spring of 1941, these versions boasting self-sealing tanks, a bullet-proof windscreen, armour protection, an uprated engine and improved armament. A total of 584 SBD-3s and 700 SBD-4s were built, and it was these machines that became the key combat aircraft in the Pacific in 1942–43. The SBD-5/6, 2,409 examples of which were built at a new Douglas plant in Oklahoma, ended the US Navy's production run for the aircraft in July 1944. The USAAC also procured nearly 900 Dauntlesses as the A-24, although they saw only limited action in the Pacific in 1942–43.

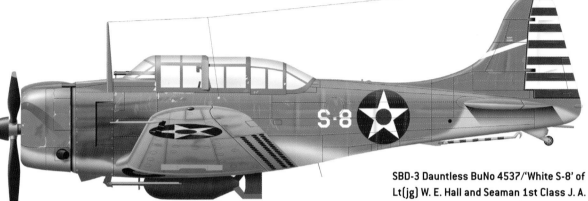

SBD-3 Dauntless BuNo 4537/'White S-8' of Lt(jg) W. E. Hall and Seaman 1st Class J. A. Moore, VS-2, USS *Lexington* (CV 2), Coral Sea, May 1942

SPECIFICATIONS (SBD-6)

Crew: Pilot and gunner

Length: 33ft (10.06m)

Wingspan: 41ft 6in (12.65m)

Height: 12ft 11in (3.94m)

Empty: 6,535lb (2,964kg)

Max T/O: 9,519lb (4,318kg)

Max Speed: 255mph (410km/h)

Range: 773 miles (1,244km)

Powerplant: Wright R-1820-66 Cyclone 9

Output: 1,350hp (1,007kW)

Armament: Two Browning 0.50in machine guns in nose and two flexibly mounted in rear cockpit; maximum bomb load of 2,250lb (1,021kg) on underwing/fuselage racks

First Flight Date: 23 July 1938 (XBT-2)

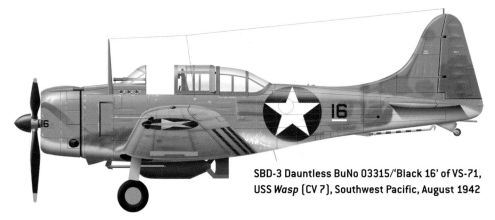

SBD-3 Dauntless BuNo 03315/'Black 16' of VS-71,
USS *Wasp* (CV 7), Southwest Pacific, August 1942

PLANE DETAILS

Previous page: Lt(jg) Hall was awarded the Medal of Honor for his 8 May 1942 action in this aircraft while defending *Lexington* from Japanese torpedo bombers during the Battle of the Coral Sea. Hall was seriously wounded in one foot but remained in the fight and shot down a B5N 'Kate'. His Dauntless was so badly shot up that it was jettisoned overboard soon after landing back aboard the doomed *Lexington*. The SBD shows typical early-war markings as worn by most carrier-based aircraft in the Pacific until mid-1942.

This page: On 25 August 1942 this SBD was used by two pilots to shoot down three Japanese aircraft. During a morning sea search Lt(jg) Chester Zalewski 'splashed' two E13A 'Jake' floatplanes from the cruisers *Atago* and *Haguro*, whilst that afternoon Lt Morris Doughty led his division against a H8K 'Emily' flying boat. Although all four SBDs in Doughty's division attacked the H8K, he was given credit for its destruction. Three documented Japanese victory flags on one SBD stood as a record.

BRISTOL BEAUFIGHTER

Built as a private venture by Bristol to overcome the RAF's embarrassing lack of long-range heavy fighters in the late 1930s, the Leslie Frise-designed Beaufighter used the wings, tail and rear fuselage of the company's rugged Beaufort torpedo bomber so as to expedite the aircraft's development. The 'minimum change' fighter that was subsequently created proved to be one of the best strike and nightfighters of World War II. Featuring a new main fuselage, powerful Bristol Hercules (and later Rolls-Royce Merlin) engines and a mixed gun and cannon armament, the prototype Beaufighter made its first flight on 17 July 1939 – barely six months after it had been conceived by Bristol's design team.

The first examples entered RAF service in September 1940, and when later fitted with radar, the Mk IF (and Merlin-powered Mk IIF) took the fight to the Luftwaffe during its nocturnal blitz of 1940–41. Further developed into the Mk VIF in 1942, this version of the Beaufighter had air intercept (AI) radar fitted in a 'thimble' nose cone. Issued to 14 fighter squadrons and four USAAF units in the Mediterranean, the Mk VIF remained an important nightfighter asset until replaced by the Mosquito (in RAF service) and P-61 Black Widow (with the USAAF) from mid-1944. By then, no fewer than 80 Allied pilots had 'made ace' flying the Beaufighter, predominantly in the nightfighting role.

The long-range dayfighter variants also proved a staple aircraft for Coastal Command, the Mk IC, VIC and TF X seeing service off the coasts of Occupied Europe from Norway to southern France, throughout the Mediterranean and North Africa and against the Japanese in the Far East. The TF X of 1943 was the definitive torpedo fighter variant, being capable of carrying an 18in or 22.5in weapon beneath its fuselage. A total of 5,584 Beaufighters were built between 1939 and 1946, including 365 in Australia. Indeed, the last aircraft built was an Australian Mk 21 in January 1946. Post-war, Beaufighters remained in frontline use with the RAF through to 1950, after which a number of TF Xs were converted into TT 10 target tugs.

Beaufighter IIF T3145 of Sqn Ldr R. M. Trousdale, No 409 Sqn RCAF, Coleby Grange, Lincolnshire, March 1942

SPECIFICATIONS (BEAUFIGHTER IF)

Crew: Pilot and navigator/radar operator/gunner

Length: 41ft 4in (12.60m)

Wingspan: 57ft 10in (17.63m)

Height: 15ft 10in (4.83m)

Empty: 14,069lb (6,382kg)

Max T/O: 21,100lb (9,571kg)

Max Speed: 323mph (520km/h)

Range: 1,170 miles (1,883km)

Powerplants: two Bristol Hercules IIIs

Output: 2,980hp (2,088kW)

Armament: Four 20mm cannon in nose and six Browning 0.303in machine guns in wings

First Flight Date: 17 July 1939

Beaufighter IC A19-40 of Sqn Ldr R. L. Gordon, No 31 Sqn RAAF, Coomalie Creek, Northern Territory, October 1943

PLANE DETAILS

Previous page: Issued new to No 409 Sqn in late 1941 when the unit swapped its Defiants for Beaufighter IIFs, this aircraft was flown both by ace Sqn Ldr Richard Trousdale and by squadron CO Wg Cdr P. Y. Davoud. Following its service with No 409 Sqn, T3145 spent time with No 456 Sqn RAAF, before being relegated to training duties with Nos 60, 132 and 54 OTUs. The fighter was written off while serving with the latter unit on 25 September 1943 when it stalled on takeoff from Charterhall, in Berwickshire, due to incorrect trimming.

This page: On 9 October 1943 future Beaufighter ace 'Butch' Gordon (with Sgt Ron Jordan as his navigator) was leading a six-aircraft attack on Selaroe Island, in the East Indies, in this machine when he was intercepted by a Ki-45 'Nick'. Gordon quickly destroyed his opponent, but a second Japanese fighter then targeted A19-40 and shot it full of holes. Jordan eventually sent this Ki-45 down too, before limping back to Livingstone strip, in Australia, and crash-landing. The Beaufighter was left fit for scrap only.

de HAVILLAND MOSQUITO

Built to replace the ageing Blenheim, the Mosquito flew very much in the face of convention by utilising a wooden fuselage and wings. Initially rejected by the Air Ministry in the autumn of 1938 on the grounds of its unorthodox construction, the aircraft's wooden structure actually ensured its series production with the outbreak of war due to the fear that the supply of light alloys from abroad would be affected by the conflict. An order for 50 aircraft was received on 1 March 1940, and the prototype Mosquito took to the skies eight months later. The sleek Merlin-powered design soon proved its worth during flight trials, possessing the manoeuvrability of a fighter and the payload of a medium bomber.

The first Mosquito to see operational service was the photo-reconnaissance variant on 20 September 1941, whilst bomber optimised B Mk IVs began to reach the frontline two months later. Whilst the Mosquito was being successfully blooded as a bomber, the prototype Mosquito fighter was already proving itself during flight trials. The first Mosquito fighter variant to see operational service was the F/NF II, which began to reach the frontline in January 1942. Over the next two years the Mosquito gradually replaced the Beaufighter as the RAF's premier nightfighter, with the radar-equipped NF XIII and NF 30 being the ultimate wartime variants – 59 pilots became aces while flying the Mosquito. In the day fighter-bomber role, the FB VI proved so successful that it became the most important Mosquito version of them all, at least in terms of numbers built (2,257 in the UK).

Numerous variant modifications were made to the overall design during its production life, which also saw the Mosquito built under-licence in Australia and Canada. Some 7,781 examples were eventually constructed, with the final aircraft, a NF 38 nightfighter, leaving de Havilland's Chester factory in November 1950. Later versions of the Mosquito remained in frontline service with the RAF through to the mid-1950s, while Training Command operated TT 38 target tugs until 1961.

Mosquito B IV DZ637 of Flg Off R. Pate and Flt Lt E. Jackson,
No 627 Sqn, Woodhall Spa, Lincolnshire, December 1944

AZ X

DZ637

SPECIFICATIONS
(MOSQUITO F II)

Crew: Pilot and navigator/radar operator

Length: 40ft 10in (12.44m)

Wingspan: 54ft 2in (16.51m)

Height: 15ft 3in (4.65m)

Empty: 14,300lb (6,486kg)

Max T/O: 20,000lb (9,072kg)

Max Speed: 370mph (595km/h)

Range: 890 miles (1,432km)

Powerplants: two Rolls-Royce Merlin 21s

Output: 2,960hp (2,506kW)

Armament: Four 20mm cannon and four
Browning 0.303in machine guns in nose

First Flight Date: 25 November 1940

Mosquito NF XIII MM571 of FLt Lt K. G. Rayment, No 264 Sqn,
B17 Caen/Carpiquet, France, September 1944

PLANE DETAILS

Previous page: One of 20 Mosquitoes modified by Marshalls and Vickers-Armstrong in 1944 to carry a 4,000lb bomb, this aircraft joined No 627 Sqn in July 1944. DZ637 flew a number of missions with the unit, including the abortive strike on the Gestapo HQ in Oslo on 31 December 1944. This aircraft was shot down over Siegen, in western Germany, on 1 February 1945.

This page: Fitted with an American-built SCR 720 (AI Mk X) centimetric search radar in a bulbous nose fairing, MM571 was delivered from the de Havilland plant at Leavesden to No 410 Sqn RCAF in the spring of 1944. Moving to France with No 264 Sqn in September of that year, the aircraft was occasionally flown by ace Ken Rayment during this period. Later transferred to No 604 Sqn, MM571 survived the war and was eventually struck off charge in January 1947.

ILYUSHIN Il-2 *SHTURMOVIK*

Built in greater numbers than any other combat aircraft in history, the Il-2 was one of the most important Soviet types fielded in action over the Eastern Front in World War II. Indeed, the units of the Red Army Air Force that were equipped with the *Shturmovik* ('armoured attacker') played a key role in defeating Germany's powerful panzer divisions on the Eastern Front and ensuring that the Wehrmacht's invasion of the USSR would ultimately fail. Developed as the Bsh-2 by Ilyushin and first flown in prototype form on 30 December 1939, the aircraft featured a heavily armoured shell for its two-man crew that formed an integral part of the machine's structure. Weighing 1,540lb, the steel shell also protected the engine and fuel tank. Although tested and initially built as a two-seater, by the time production aircraft started to reach frontline units March 1941 the Il-2 (as it was now designated) had lost the rear gunner's position.

A considerable number of aircraft were serving with the various Soviet air forces by the time Germany invaded the USSR in June 1941 thanks to production from three large manufacturing plants that averaged 1,200 Il-2s per month throughout World War II. Armed with two VYa-23 23mm cannon, highly effective RS-82 and ROFS-132 high-explosive rocket projectiles and FAB-100 bombs, the aircraft proved deadly against marauding Wehrmacht Panzers as pairs of Il-2s roamed the frontline at low level. However, the *Shturmoviks* were in turn highly vulnerable to attack from the rear by enemy fighters, so Ilyushin was ordered to revert to the two-seat layout – with a UBT 12.7mm machine gun for the rear gunner – in September 1942 with production of the Il-2M.

The vastly improved Il-10 replaced the Il-2 on the production lines from October 1944, the new machine being more streamlined thanks to wheels that turned to lie flush in the revised, lighter wings. It also had an all-stressed-skin structure, a more powerful version of the venerable Mikulin AM V12 engine, improved armour and better armament. More than 43,100 Il-2/10s were built between 1941 and 1955.

Il-2 *Shturmovik* of 667th ShAP (Attack Air Regiment),
Kalinin Front, northern Russia, January 1943

SPECIFICATIONS (II-2M)

Crew: Pilot and rear gunner

Length: 39ft 4.50in (12m)

Wingspan: 47ft 11in (14.60m)

Height: 11ft 1.75in (3.40m)

Empty: 7,165lb (3,250kg)

Max T/O: 12,947lb (5,872kg)

Max Speed: 281mph (449km/h)

Range: 373 miles (600km)

Powerplant: Mikulin AM-38F

Output: 1,750hp (1,305kW)

Armament: Two VYa 23mm cannon in wings and one manually-aimed UBT 12.7mm machine gun in rear cockpit; maximum bomb/rocket load of 1,323lb (600kg) on underwing racks

First Flight Date: 30 December 1939

Il-2M *Shturmovik* of 6th GShAP, 1st Baltic Front, January 1945

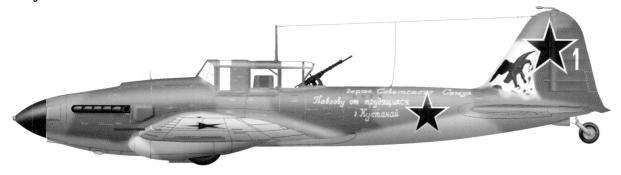

PLANE DETAILS

Previous page: The members of Moscow-based Yaroslavl Komsomol Factory No 30 bought a whole squadron of Il-2s, and the suitably decorated winter camouflaged aircraft were in turn handed over to the best pilots of 667th ShAP, 292nd ShAD (Attack Air Division), 1st ShAK (Attack Air Corps) in early 1943. The regiment became 141st GShAP (Guards Attack Air Regiment) in Order 016 of the People's Commissar of Defence, dated 5 February 1944.

This page: The inscription displayed on this aircraft reads 'To the Hero of Soviet Union Pavlov from the workers of Kustanay town'. Upon its arrival in the frontline, the Il-2 had been presented to two-time Hero of the Soviet Union Capt I. F. Pavlov, who was then a squadron leader in 6th GShAP. Pavlov subsequently saw action in this aircraft when his regiment targeted enemy forces in East Prussia during the Red Army assault on Königsberg (now Kaliningrad) in April 1945.

NAKAJIMA Ki-43 HAYABUSA

The staple Japanese Army Air Force (JAAF) fighter of World War II, the Ki-43 was produced in greater numbers than any of its land-based contemporaries. Developed as a direct replacement for Nakajima's Ki-27, the Hayabusa (Peregrine) embraced the same design philosophy in that it was built to be supremely manoeuvrable at the expense of effective armament, protection for the pilot and structural strength. Following the delivery of ten service trials aircraft in 1939–40 (which were criticised by JAAF test pilots for not being as agile as the Ki-27), production Ki-43-Is began to arrive in the frontline in the spring of 1941. Three sub-variants of the two-bladed -I were produced between April 1941 and February 1943, all of which featured different armament.

The Hayabusa made its combat debut with the 59th and 64th Sentais during the Japanese invasion of Southeast Asia in December 1941, and flying alongside the more numerous Ki-27, it swiftly cleared the skies of Allied opposition. Many pilots achieved ace status in the Ki-43 during this early period of the conflict. Light weight and a large wing area gave the fighter (codenamed 'Oscar' by the Allies) a smaller turning radius and higher rate of climb than its opponents. On the other hand, it lacked firepower, armour and fuel tank protection, and its structure, while not fragile, could not absorb much punishment. Furthermore, it could be out-dived by most Allied fighters. Pilots also complained that the Ki-43-I was underpowered.

Nakajima responded with production of the re-engined Ki-43-II of late 1943. Aside from the fitment of the supercharged Nakajima Ha-115 radial engine, the new fighter employed a three-bladed constant speed propeller. The Ki-43-II also had reduced-span 'clipped' wings, strengthened underwing hardpoints, limited pilot armour and a revised windscreen and canopy. Although the Ki-43-II/III was outclassed by Allied fighters like the P-47 and P-38 by the time it reached the frontline, the aircraft remained in production to war's end, by which time 5,919 examples had been built.

Ki-43-I Hayabusa of Maj Katsuji Sugiura, CO of the 11th Sentai,
Mingaladon, Burma, November 1942

SPECIFICATIONS
(Ki-43-IIB)

Crew: Pilot

Length: 29ft 3.25in (8.92m)

Wingspan: 35ft 6.75in (10.84m)

Height: 10ft 8.75in (3.27m)

Empty: 4,211lb (1,910kg)

Max T/O: 6,450lb (2,926kg)

Max Speed: 329mph (529km/h)

Range: 1,095 miles (1,762km)

Powerplant: Nakajima Ha-115

Output: 1,150hp (857kW)

Armament: Two Ho-103 12.7mm machine guns
in nose; maximum bomb load of 1,102lb (500kg)
on underwing racks

First Flight Date: January 1939

Ki-43-II Hayabusa of WO Akira Sugimoto, 54th Sentai/3rd Chutai, Fabrica, Negros Island, the Philippines, January 1945

PLANE DETAILS

Previous page: The two bold white bands behind this aircraft's cockpit indicate that this garish Ki-43-I (featuring lightning bolts in all three chutai colours on the tail) was assigned to the sentai CO, Maj Katsuji Sugiura. He led the unit, known as the 'Lightning Sentai', from March 1942 until he was killed in action on 6 February 1943 in New Guinea.

This page: This aircraft displays the sentai insignia, its application in yellow denoting that its assignment to the 3rd Chutai. Having been an instructor for several years, Sugimoto was one of the most experienced Ki-43 pilots in the Philippines by early 1945. On 7 January he was shot down in this aircraft by P-38 pilot Lt Douglas Thropp. Having survived the crash-landing, Sugimoto was slain in the cockpit of his Hayabusa by Filipino partisans.

MARTIN B-26 MARAUDER

Martin relied on its previous experience as a successful bomber builder for the USAAC when it entered its Model 179 in the widely contested 1939 Medium Bomber competition. The army was looking for an aircraft that had good speed, range and ceiling performance, was armed with four 0.30in guns and could carry 2,000lb of bombs. It did not specify optimum landing speeds, and understood that long takeoff runs would be required. In order to meet the specifications stipulated by the requirement, Martin built its Model 179 around a wing optimised for high-speed cruising rather than moderate landing speeds.

Far in advance of its competitors in terms of performance and potential production, the Martin bomber easily won the competition in September 1939 and 201 examples were ordered straight 'off the drawing board'. However, the manufacturer's decision to plumb for high wing loading resulted in an aircraft that initially proved difficult for novice pilots to fly safely. The B-26 (as it was designated by the USAAC

upon its entry into service in the spring of 1941) soon earned an unenviable reputation as a 'widow maker'. Converting crews onto the aircraft proved a lengthy, and often dangerous, process, and despite Martin improving the bomber's handling characteristics (from the 641st B-model onwards) through the fitment of a greater wingspan and taller tail, the sobriquet remained with the B-26 throughout its service career.

In light of this, it is therefore ironic that the Marauder enjoyed the lowest loss rate of any USAAF bomber to see action in the European theatre – B-26s equipped eight bomb groups in the ETO and MTO between 1943–45. The Marauder also saw widespread use in the Pacific, the type having made its combat debut in this theatre in April 1942. Although not used in combat, the US Navy was also supplied with 272 Marauders (designated JM-1/2s) for use as target tugs, while the 522 Marauder I/II/IIIs assigned to the RAF and South African Air Force saw action in North Africa and Italy from 1942. The last of 5,157 B-26s built by Martin was delivered on 28 April 1945.

B-26B-40-MA Marauder 42-43278 of the 37th BS/17th BG,
Villacidro, Sardinia, August 1944

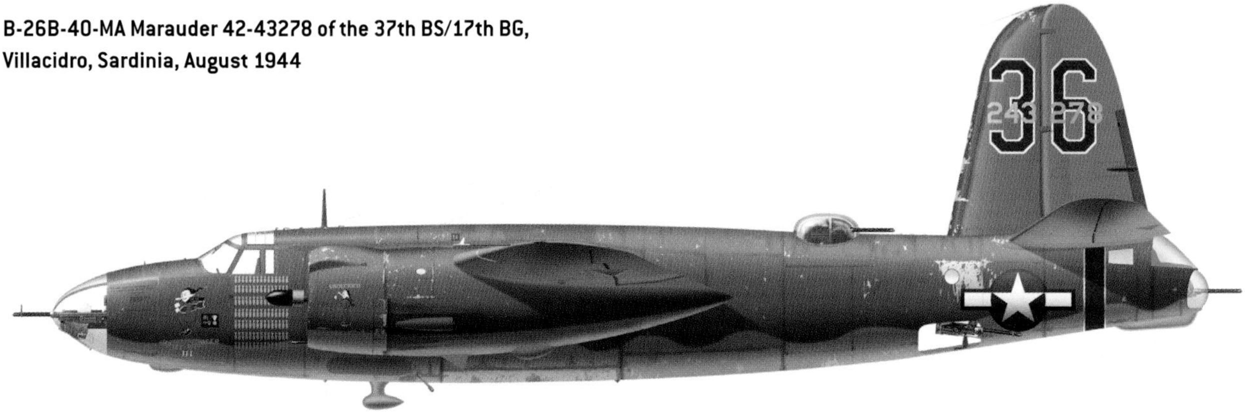

SPECIFICATIONS (B-26G)

Crew: Pilot, co-pilot, bombardier/nose gunner, radio operator, navigator, dorsal and tail turret gunners

Length: 56ft 1in (17.09m)

Wingspan: 71ft (21.64 m)

Height: 20ft 4in (6.20m)

Empty: 25,300lb (11,476kg)

Max T/O: 38,200lb (17,327kg)

Max Speed: 283mph (455km/h)

Range: 1,100 miles (1,770km)

Powerplant: two Pratt & Whitney R-2800-43 Double Wasps

Output: 3,840hp (2,684kW)

Armament: Four fixed Browning 0.50in machine guns on fuselage sides, one in nose, pairs in dorsal and tail turrets and two in ventral positions; maximum bomb load of 4,000lb (1,814kg) in bomb-bay

First Flight Date: 25 November 1940

B-26G-5-MA Marauder 43-34284 of the 442nd BS/320th BG, Longvic, France, January 1945

PLANE DETAILS

Previous page: *JERSEY BOUNCER III* was in service with the 17th BG from 12 September 1943 through to 17 December 1944, when it was shot down by flak whilst attacking defensive positions along the 'Siegfried Line' – its pilot on that day was 1Lt Donald V. Leslie. On 2 July, 42-43278 had become the first B-26 from the 17th BG to complete 100 missions, and it had boosted its tally to 130 by the time of its demise.

This page: *Green Eyed Glodine* was named by its regular pilot, 1Lt Robert A. Perrine, in honour of his wife, Glodine. F/G-model Marauders were a big improvement over earlier versions of the bomber, with their primary design change being a 3.5-degree increase to the wing incidence. Despite a slight decrease in speed, this change gave a shorter takeoff run and better handling that would have saved the lives of many previous crews.

LOCKHEED P-38 LIGHTNING

The P-38 Lightning was Lockheed's first venture into the world of high performance military aircraft. Keen to break into this lucrative military marketplace, the company had eagerly responded to the USAAC's 1937 Request for Proposals pertaining to the acquisition of a long-range interceptor. The new machine had to have a top speed in excess of 360mph at 20,000ft, the ability to takeoff and land over a 50ft obstacle within 2,200ft, the reliability to fly at full throttle for over an hour non-stop and boast an armament double that of the P-36A Hawk – the USAAC's frontline fighter of the period.

No aircraft then in service, or under development, with any air arm across the globe could match these performance figures, and Lockheed's design team, led by H. L. Hibbard and Clarence 'Kelly' Johnson, soon realised that any new type proposed by them would have to be twin-engined in order to allow the fighter to attain the top speed or rate of climb stipulated by the specification. The powerplant chosen for the fighter was the 960hp Allison V-1710, as used by its P-40

contemporary. Aside from its novel twin-boom and central nacelle layout, the prototype XP-38 utilised butt-joined and flush-riveted all-metal skins and flying surfaces – a first for a US fighter. The XP-38's test programme progressed well, and aside from some minor adjustments to the flying surfaces and introduction of progressively more powerful Allison engines, frontline P-38s (of which 10,036 were built up to August 1945) differed little from the prototype throughout the aircraft's six-year production run.

The appellation 'Lightning' was bestowed upon the P-38 by the RAF and adopted by the Americans with advent of the E-model in mid-1941. The definitive P-38 models – namely the E, F, H, J and L – fitted with supercharged Allison engines, improved Fowler flaps and extra fuel, proved more than a match for Axis fighters across the globe. Indeed, the Lightning was credited with more kills in the Pacific theatre than any other USAAF type, and the two top scoring American pilots of World War II claimed all their victories with P-38s.

P-38G-1 Lightning 42-12705 of 1Lt C. Homer, 80th FS/8rh FG,
Port Moresby, New Guinea, November 1943

SPECIFICATIONS (P-38J)

Crew: Pilot

Length: 37ft 10in (11.53m)

Wingspan: 52ft (15.85m)

Height: 9ft 10in (3m)

Empty: 12,780lb (5,797kg)

Max T/O: 21,600lb (9,798kg)

Max Speed: 414mph (666km/h)

Range: 475 miles (764km)

Powerplant: two Allison V-1710-89s

Output: 2,850hp (2,126kW)

Armament: One AN-M2 'C' 20mm cannon and four
Browning 0.50in machine guns in nose;
maximum bomb/rocket load of 3,200lb
(1,451kg) under wings

First Flight Date: 27 January 1939

P-38L-5 (serial unknown) of Capt B. DeHaven, 7th FS/49th FG,
Tacloban, Leyte, November 1944

PLANE DETAILS

Previous page: This aircraft was the first P-38G-1 assigned to future 15-kill ace Cy Homer upon his arrival in the Southwest Pacific, the aircraft having been supplied new to the 80th FS in Australia in early 1943. Variously named *COTTON DUSTER*, *aVa* and *LILLY NELL* by its pilot and groundcrew, 42-12705 was routinely flown by Homer throughout 1943 – he claimed two kills and three probables with it.

This page: Bob DeHaven enjoyed himself in the target rich skies over Leyte in the autumn of 1944. He claimed four kills and one damaged between 29 October and 4 November, and all of these victories were almost certainly achieved in this P-38L-5. The 7th FS's Bunyip emblem adorns the fighter's twin fins, this marking being synonymous with the unit's spell in Darwin defending northern Australia in 1942. DeHaven's fighter was reportedly destroyed in an enemy bombing raid soon after he had returned home on leave in mid November.

FOCKE-WULF Fw 190

The Fw 190 caught the RAF by surprise when it first appeared over the Channel front in 1941, and it remained unmatched in aerial combat until the advent of the Spitfire Mk IX in late 1942. Powered by the compact BMW 801 radial engine, the Fw 190 boasted excellent handling characteristics to match its turn of speed. The A-model Fw 190 was the dedicated fighter variant, and as the design matured so more guns were fitted and more power squeezed out of the BMW engine. By the end of 1942, production of the Fw 190 accounted for half of all German fighters built that year, and the fighter-bomber F/G had also been developed – F-models entered frontline service on the Eastern Front during the winter of 1942–43. All manner of ordnance from bombs to rockets could be carried by the fighter-bomber Fw 190, and additional protective armour for the pilot was also added around the cockpit. Variants of the Fw 190 saw action against the Allies on all fronts of the war in Europe, and the aircraft remained a deadly opponent until VE-Day.

Developed in 1942 as a replacement for the aborted Fw 190B/C high altitude fighters, the *Langnasen-Dora* (Longnose-Dora) made use of the inverted inline Junkers Jumo 213 engine, combined with an MW50 water/methanol booster, to achieve an impressive rate of climb and top speed. In contrast to the many models and sub-variants of the Fw 190A/F/G, only the D-9 version of the 'Dora' was produced in large numbers.

Service entry was achieved in August 1944, and the first fighters to reach the *Jagdwaffe* were employed as Me 262 airfield defenders. A number of D-9s participated in the last ditch *Bodenplatte* operation staged at dawn on New Year's Day 1945 against numerous Allied airfields in Western Europe, and the survivors of this mission were later absorbed within the Defence of the Reich force. In February 1945 production commenced on the D-12, which was equipped with an uprated Jumo 213 F-1 engine, a 30mm cannon firing through the nose and better protective armour for the pilot, but only a handful were built before Germany surrendered in May 1945.

Fw 190A-4 'White Chevron and Triangle' of Hauptmann E. Mayer,
Gruppenkommandeur III./JG 2, Cherbourg-Théville, France,
February 1943

SPECIFICATIONS
(Fw 190A-3)

Crew: Pilot

Length: 29ft (8.84m)

Wingspan: 34ft 5.5in (10.50m)

Height: 13ft (3.96m)

Empty: 6,393lb (2,900kg)

Max T/O: 8,770lb (3,978kg)

Max Speed: 382mph (615km/h)

Range: 497 miles (800km)

Powerplant: BMW 801D

Output: 1,700hp (1,268kW)

Armament: Two 7.9mm machine guns in nose
and four 20mm cannon in wings

First Flight Date: 1 June 1939

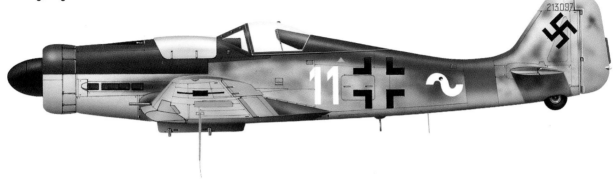

Fw 190D-9 'White 11' of 13./JG 51, Flensburg, Germany, May 1945

PLANE DETAILS

Previous page: Egon Mayer's A-4 displays a wealth of markings, including the 'Cockerel's head' *Gruppe* badge, stylised black panel surrounding the engine exhaust louvres, a *Kommandeur's* white geometric 'Chevron and triangle' symbol and, behind the fuselage Balkenkreuz, the thin band – also white outlined in black – which III./JG 2 used to identify its *Gruppenstab* machines. Like many of JG 2's *Experten*, Mayer kept a detailed record of his victories on the rudder of his aircraft.

This page: In mid-April 1945 IV./JG 51 received at least six Fw 190D-9s. After briefly operating with 13. and 14. *Staffeln*, all but one or two of these machines were flown from Parchim/Redlin to Flensburg on 2 May to await IV./JG 51's surrender to British forces. In the final three weeks of combat defending Berlin from bases directly east of the besieged German capital, the *Gruppe* had claimed 115 enemy aircraft shot down for the loss of just five Fw 190s.

HAWKER TYPHOON

The Typhoon was the first fighter to enter RAF service that was capable of achieving speeds in excess of 400mph in level flight. However, the brutish Hawker fighter was almost deemed a failure right at the start of its career when the combination of poor climb and altitude performance, unreliability of its new Napier Sabre and suspect rear fuselage assembly cast serious doubts over its suitability for frontline service. Refusing to give up on the design, Hawker and Napier spent more than a year (from mid-1941 through to mid-1942) 'beefing up' the airframe and correcting engine maladies to the point where the Typhoon was found to be an excellent low altitude fighter. Pilots flying the Hawker machine claimed 246 victories as they effectively blunted the Luftwaffe's Fw 190 'hit and run' raiders, who frequently terrorised the south coast of England in 1942–43.

Its proven ability at low-level also made the Typhoon the RAF's chosen heavyweight fighter-bomber to support the British and Canadian armies during the invasion of north-west Europe. Indeed, the 20 squadrons equipped with the aircraft in the 2nd Tactical Air Force (TAF) should appear in any list of 'war-winners'. They introduced the large-scale use of the rocket projectile to land battles, performed the main role in taking out the German radar defence systems prior to D-Day, made the key intervention in defeating the almost-successful German counter-attack at Mortain in August 1944 and undertook pinpoint attacks on enemy headquarters that crippled the Wehrmacht's ability to respond at key periods in 1944–45. These battles were by no means one-sided, however, with the Typhoon's nemesis – the highly effective German flak units – exacting a terrible toll on 2nd TAF units from June 1944 through to the war's end. Indeed, some 400 aircraft and 150 pilots were lost during the Normandy campaign alone.

Of the 3,330 Typhoons delivered to the RAF between July 1941 and November 1945, no fewer than 3,315 were constructed by Gloster. Surviving examples were quickly replaced by Spitfires and Tempest Vs post-war.

Typhoon IB JP649 of No 247 Sqn, No 124 Airfield, Merston,
West Sussex, November 1943

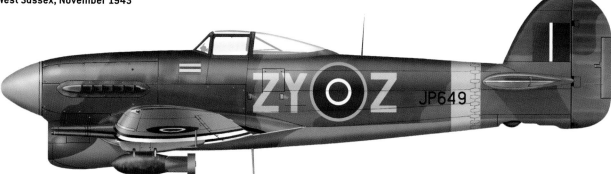

SPECIFICATIONS
(TYPHOON IB)

Crew: Pilot

Length: 31ft 11in (9.73m)

Wingspan: 41ft 7in (12.67m)

Height: 15ft 3.5in (4.66m)

Empty: 9,800lb (4,445kg)

Max T/O: 13,980lb (6,341kg)

Max Speed: 405mph (652km/h)

Range: 610 miles (982km)

Powerplant: Napier Sabre IIA

Output: 2,180hp (1,626kW)

Armament: Four 20mm cannon in wings;
provision for two 500lb (227kg) or 1,000lb
(454kg) bombs or eight 3in/60lb (7.62cm/27kg)
rockets under wings

First Flight Date: 24 February 1940

Typhoon IB MN601 of No 245 Sqn, No 121 Wing, RAF Holmsley South, Hampshire, June 1944

PLANE DETAILS

Previous page: When Sqn Ldr Erik Haabjorn took command of No 247 Sqn in late August 1943, he adopted JP649 as 'Z', his personal aircraft. The squadron started flying bomber operations in early November of that same year, and Haabjorn flew the aircraft until the beginning of January 1944, when it was replaced by JR449, fitted with a sliding hood. JP649 was lost on a long-range sweep to Chateaudun on 14 February 1944. Its pilot, Flg Off A. S. Aitchison, was killed.

This page: Flg Off Bill Smith made the first wheels down landing on the first RAF Advanced Landing Ground in the Normandy beachhead in this aircraft. MN601 had been delivered to No 245 Sqn just days earlier, the fighter remaining with the unit until damaged in action on 31 July 1944. Once repaired it was then allocated to No 263 Sqn. In March 1945 MN601 was overhauled by Marshall of Cambridge, but the fighter saw no further service and was sold for scrap in 1947.

CONSOLIDATED B-24 LIBERATOR

Born out of an approach made by the USAAC to Consolidated for a bomber with superior performance to the B-17, the Liberator was built in near record time. Designated the Model 32 by its manufacturer, the bomber was designed around the then-new long-span/low-drag Davis wing. In March 1939 the army ordered 36 production examples before the prototype XB-24 had even flown – a French purchasing mission also bought 120 bombers, these aircraft being issued to Britain following France's defeat by Germany in June 1940. Indeed, it was the British who coined the name 'Liberator', RAF Coastal Command aircraft being the first of the type to see action, over the Atlantic, in June 1941. That same month the USAAC received its first B-24As, although these machines were used almost exclusively by the Air Corps' Ferry Command.

Indeed, it was not until the advent of the B-24D in early 1942 that a true heavy bomber version of the Liberator finally went into series production. This variant featured self-sealing fuel tanks, extra defensive armour and the fitment of turbocharged Pratt & Whitney Twin Wasp R-1830-41 engines. Production soon got into full swing, and it was the D-model which was sent to the Middle East, the Pacific and Europe in late 1942 to wage war against Axis forces.

Built on five productions lines by Consolidated (San Diego and Fort Worth), Douglas (Tulsa), Ford (Willow Run) and North American (Dallas), the most successful B-24 variant of them all was the J-model – no fewer than 6,678 were completed between 1943–45. Some 977 Liberators were also used by the US Navy as land-based patrol bombers in PB4Y form both in the Pacific and Europe. The RAF received 1,694 examples across a handful of mark numbers, its Liberators seeing combat in Europe, the Mediterranean and the Far East. By the time production ceased on 31 May 1945, 18,475 Liberators had been built, making it the most produced American aircraft of World War II. The USAAF declared its B-24s surplus at war's end, but the US Navy kept its PB4Y-1Ps in service until 1951.

B-24D-25-CO Liberator 41-24223 of the 373rd BS/308th BG, Yangkai, China, October–November 1943

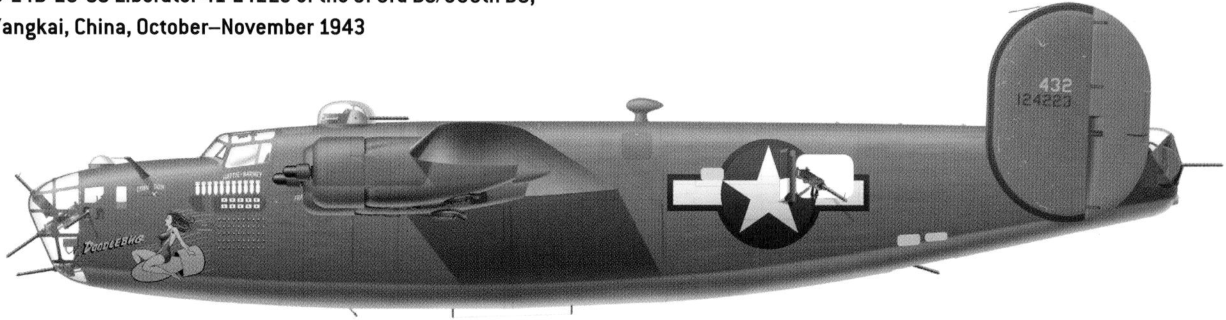

SPECIFICATIONS (B-24J)

Crew: Pilot and co-pilot, flight engineer, navigator, bombardier/nose gunner, radio operator/dorsal gunner, two waist gunners, ball turret gunner and tail gunner

Length: 67ft 2in (20.47m)

Wingspan: 110ft (33.53m)

Height: 18ft (5.49m)

Empty: 36,500lb (16,556kg)

Max T/O: 71,200lb (32,296kg)

Max Speed: 290mph (467km/h)

Range: 2,100 miles (3,380km)

Powerplant: four Pratt & Whitney R-1830-65 Twin Wasps

Output: 4,800hp (3,580kW)

Armament: Nose, tail, dorsal and ball turrets equipped with two Browning 0.50in machine guns, and two guns in waist; maximum bomb load of 12,000lb (5,443kg) in bomb-bay/inner wing racks

First Flight Date: 29 December 1939

B-24M-15-CO Liberator 44-42133 of the 374th BS/308th BG, Chengkung, China, early summer 1945

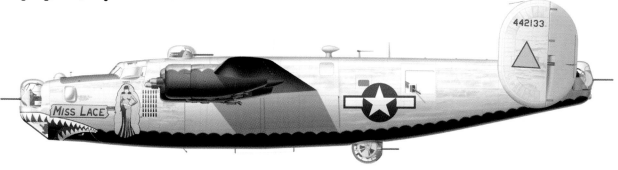

PLANE DETAILS

Previous page: A San Diego-built D-model, *Doodlebug* was one of the original nine B-24Ds assigned to the 373rd BS in February 1943. During the bomber's ten months in-theatre, it flew 11 bombing missions and more than 50 sorties over the Himalayan 'Hump' ferrying gasoline, bombs and other supplies for the 308th. 41-24223 was sent home in December 1943 in company with fellow 308th BG veterans *THE MIGHTY EIGHTBALL*, *The Pelican* and *Snowball From Hell*.

This page: A Consolidated-built M-model delivered on 19 January 1945, *Miss Lace* was named after the famous character in Milton Caniff's wartime comic strip 'Male Call'. It flew 34 combat missions and claimed two ships sunk. When the 308th BG ceased bombing missions in the summer of 1945, *Miss Lace* had its armament removed and was tasked (along with other Liberators) with hauling fuel over the 'Hump' in bomb-bay tanks. The bomber returned to the USA at the end of 1945 for disposal.

REPUBLIC P-47 THUNDERBOLT

The original P-47 design was produced to meet a 1940 USAAC requirement for a lightweight interceptor similar in size and stature to the Spitfire and Bf 109. Powered by Allison's V-1710-39 1,150hp inline engine, the XP-47A had just two 0.50in machine guns as armament and lacked protective armour or self-sealing tanks. However, combat reports from Europe proved the folly of a lightweight fighter, and the USAAC modified its design requirements to include an eight-gun fitment, heavy armour plating and a self-sealing fuel system. Republic responded with an all-new design, powered, crucially, by a turbocharged R-2800 Double Wasp radial engine. Despite initial reliability problems with this motor, production of the Republic design forged ahead.

In late 1942 the 56th FG gave the P-47B its combat debut with the Eighth Air Force in England, the group performing vital escort missions for B-17 bombers. Initial encounters with German fighters were not encouraging for Thunderbolt pilots, as their mount was outmanoeuvred at low to medium altitudes and its engine performance was lacklustre – the aircraft's short range was also criticised. The arrival of the C-model in mid-1943 addressed these problems, and as combat tactics evolved, pilots learned how best to fly the Thunderbolt in order to effectively counter the more nimble Luftwaffe fighters. By the end of 1943, the first D-models had reached the UK, followed five months later by 'bubble top' Thunderbolts, which became the favoured mount thanks to their superior rearward visibility.

Aside from its use as a bomber escort, the Thunderbolt also performed great work as a fighter-bomber in the ETO, MTO and the Pacific. The ultimate Thunderbolt was the P-47N, whose uprated turbocharged R-2800-61 engine was capable of producing 2,800hp in combat configuration at 32,500ft. Some 1,816 P-47Ns were built (out of a total of 15,677 Thunderbolts in total), the majority of which were put to use escorting B-29s on bombing raids on the Japanese home islands in 1945. A number of P-47Ns soldiered on with the Air National Guard, and a handful of other air arms, into the early 1950s.

P-47C-5 Thunderbolt 41-6325 of Lt J. Vogt, 63rd FS/56th FG, Halesworth, Suffolk, October 1943

SPECIFICATIONS (P-47D-25)

Crew: Pilot

Length: 36ft 1.75in (11.02m)

Wingspan: 40ft 9.25in (12.43m)

Height: 14ft 2in (4.32m)

Empty: 10,000lb (4,536kg)

Max T/O: 19,400lb (8,800kg)

Max Speed: 428mph (688km/h)

Range: 475 miles (760km)

Powerplant: Pratt & Whitney R-2800-59 Double Wasp

Output: 2,300hp (1,715kW)

Armament: Eight Browning 0.50in machine guns wings in wings; maximum bomb/rocket load of 1,000lb (454kg) on underwing racks

First Flight Date: 6 May 1941 (XP-47B)

P-47D-25 Thunderbolt 42-26641 of Col D. Schilling,
CO of the 56th FG, Boxted, Essex, December 1944

PLANE DETAILS

Previous page: John Vogt was one of a number Eighth Air Force aces to claim victories flying the same type of aircraft with more than one group – in his case the 56th and 356th FGs. 41-6325 was Vogt's first assigned aircraft in the 56th, and he used it to score his first three victories before moving on to a P-47D-10. Surviving for almost two years in the frontline, 41-6325 was eventually damaged beyond repair during combat on 20 April 1945.

This page: One of seven P-47s assigned to Dave Schilling during his time with the 56th FG, this fighter revealed an early 'Wolfpack' penchant for painting 'Dogpatch' cartoon characters on its Thunderbolts by featuring a neat rendering of 'Hairless Joe' on its cowling. Schilling's penultimate aircraft (he was subsequently issued with P-47M-1 44-21125, but engine problems saw it grounded), this D-25 was used by the colonel for his 'five in a day' haul on 23 December 1944, raising his final tally to 22.5 aerial victories.

KAWASAKI Ki-61 HIEN

One of the few examples of successful Axis material cooperation in World War II, the Kawasaki Ha-40 inline engine was a lightened development of the excellent Daimler-Benz DB 601A inverted V12 inline motor. The fighter designed specifically to utilise this powerplant was the sleek Ki-61 Hein (Flying Swallow) which, aside from having an inline rather than a more traditional radial engine, also boasted a high wing loading, armour protection for the pilot and self-sealing tanks – all things rarely associated with Japanese combat aircraft of the period. While the fighter could not hope to emulate the agility of the Ki-43, tending to stall and spin out to port with any overly violent use of the ailerons and rudder, the Ki-61 still retained a measure of traditional manoeuvrability. It responded quickly and positively to smooth use of the controls, and the Hein could hold its own in a dive against its heavier US opponents.

The fighter made its combat debut over the jungles of New Guinea in April 1943, and it soon proved itself to be more than a match for Allied P-38s, P-39s and P-40s. The Ki-61 (known as the 'Tony' to Allied pilots) was quickly plagued by engine problems, which together with other factors, and despite the valiant efforts of its pilots, seriously impeded its undoubted impact on the campaign. Used operationally on other fronts, but only in small numbers, the Hein never achieved its expected potential. During the air defence of Japan, however, it became the equipment of several elite fighter units.

In production until the war's end, the K-61 was the subject of many improvements, both in respect to its armament (which was increased through the fitment of cannon and bomb racks) and the power output of its Kawasaki engine. The resulting Ki-61-II-KAI had a performance to rival any of its piston-engined contemporaries, especially at altitude. Production of the II-KAI commenced in September 1944, but the combination of chronic powerplant problems and a devastating B-29 raid on the Kawasaki engine works meant that only 99 of the 374 airframes completed received the definitive Ha-140 V12.

**Ki-61-I-Tei Hien of section leader Lt Tohru Shinomiya,
244th Sentai *Shinten Seiku Tai*, Chofu, Tokyo, December 1944**

SPECIFICATIONS (Ki-61-I)

Crew: Pilot

Length: 28ft 8.5in (8.75m)

Wingspan: 39ft 4.5in (12m)

Height: 12ft 2in (3.71m)

Empty: 4,872lb (2,210kg)

Max T/O: 7,165lb (3,250kg)

Max Speed: 368mph (592km/h)

Range: 684 miles (1,100km)

Powerplant: Kawasaki Ha-40

Output: 1,175hp (876kW)

Armament: Two 12.7mm machine guns in nose and two in wings

First Flight Date: December 1941

Ki-61-I-Tei Hien of the 55th Sentai, Sano, Osaka, late March 1945

PLANE DETAILS

Previous page: Featuring the 244th's distinctive all-red tail marking, this aircraft has been personalised through the addition of the first syllable of the pilot's surname phonetically in white on the rudder. A section of this machine's left wing was lost in a ramming attack on a B-29 over Tokyo on 3 December 1944, although Shinomiya still managed to landing safely at Chofu. Decorated following this exploit, Shinomiya later perished on 29 April 1945 while leading a suicide attack on Okinawa.

This page: The 55th Sentai, armed exclusively with the Ki-61, was formed at Taisho airfield in March 1944. As part of the 18th Fighter Division, its main duty was home defence. Having briefly seen action in the Philippines in late 1944, the unit achieved no spectacular results defending Japan. Aircraft '37' was based at Sano, on the eastern coast of Osaka Bay, south-west of Osaka city.

MACCHI C.202 FOLGORE

One of Italy's best fighters in World War II, the C.202 could trace its lineage back to the popular C.200 Saetta of the late 1930s. Whilst the C.200 had been a solid and reliable fighter, it had always suffered from a lack of straightline speed. To solve this problem, Macchi turned away from home-grown radial engines for the Saetta's replacement, instead choosing to use Daimler-Benz's excellent DB 601A inline engine as proven in the Bf 109E. The resulting fighter was 60mph faster than the C.200, possessed a superior rate of climb and could cruise at altitudes in excess of 37,500ft. There was little degradation of the Saetta's excellent handling qualities either. Designated the C.202 Folgore ('Thunderbolt'), initial production aircraft reached the frontline in July 1941 fitted with imported German engines, but the remaining 800+ were equipped with the licence-built Alfa Romeo RA.1000 RC41-1 Monsone version of the Daimler-Benz powerplant.

Unfortunately for pilots, Macchi, as with the Saetta, once again restricted armament to just two 12.7mm machine guns, although late-build examples were also fitted with two additional guns in the wings and, in one batch, 20mm cannon under them. A fighter-bomber variant in the form of the C.202CB was also produced, whilst those tropicalised (through the fitment of a sand filter) were known as C.202ASs.

The Folgore quickly proved superior to both the Hurricane II and P-40 Tomahawk/Kittyhawk during its first North African engagements in the autumn of 1941, and examples flown by as many as 19 *gruppi* would later see action over the Balkans, the Western Desert, Sicily, the Eastern Front and Malta. Most of Italy's ranking aces scored the bulk of their victories in the C.202. However, the combination of combat losses, relatively low production rates and poor serviceability meant that the number of C.202s available to frontline units was far less than required.

Like the C.200, the Folgore also served in modest numbers on both sides after the Italian surrender, and production of the fighter continued until 1944.

C.202 Folgore *Serie* III MM7720 of Capitano Franco Lucchini,
CO of 84ª *Squadriglia*, 10° *Gruppo*, 4° *Stormo*, Fuka, Egypt,
September 1942

SPECIFICATIONS (C.202)

Crew: Pilot

Length: 29ft 0.5in (8.85m)

Wingspan: 34ft 8.5in (10.58m)

Height: 9ft 11.5in (3.03m)

Empty: 5,545lb (2,515kg)

Max T/O: 6,766lb (3,069kg)

Max Speed: 372mph (598km/h)

Range: 475 miles (764km)

Powerplant: Alfa Romeo RA.1000 RC41-1 Monsone
(Daimler-Benz DB 601A)

Output: 1,175hp (876kW)

Two 12.7mm machine guns in nose; later aircraft
had additional two 7.7mm machine guns in wings,
some with two 20mm cannon under wings

First Flight Date: 10 August 1940

C.202 *Serie* III MM7944 of Tenente Giulio Reiner, CO of 73ᵃ
Squadriglia, 9° *Gruppo*, 4° *Stormo*, Fuka, Egypt, August 1942

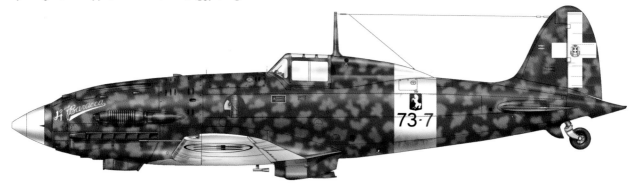

PLANE DETAILS

Previous page: A long-lived machine that had originally been issued new to 1° *Stormo* during the autumn of 1941, by this stage in its career MM7720 had had its starboard wing replaced by a flying surface from a later C.202. Assigned to 84ᵃ *Squadriglia* in early September 1942, this machine was flown regularly by 21-victory ace Capitano Lucchini during the battle of El Alamein.

This page: This aircraft's camouflage consists of mottling applied in Nocciola Chiaro (tan) over a Verde Oliva Scuro (olive green) base. Note that MM7944 has white wingtips to denote its assignment to the North African theatre. Barely visible on its fin are two kill markings. Reiner claimed seven victories between May and December 1942, a number of them in MM7944.

NORTH AMERICAN P-51 MUSTANG

The Mustang has its origins in a British Purchasing Commission deal struck with North American in April 1940 for an advanced fighter to supplant the Spitfire, the company having a completed prototype ready for flight within 120 days of the original submission. The prototype was completed just three days short of the required date, the aircraft (christened the 'Mustang I' by the British) handling beautifully in testing thanks to its revolutionary semi-laminar flow airfoil wing. However, it was soon realised that the fighter's Allison V-1710 performed poorly above 17,000ft due to its lack of supercharging, so RAF Mustang Is were fitted with cameras and relegated to the low-level tactical reconnaissance and army co-operation roles. The USAAF, seeing that the Mustang I was no good as a fighter above medium altitude, ordered just 500 A-36As and 310 P-51As for ground attack tasks instead.

Although the Mustang I's performance had let it down in high-altitude dogfights, the airframe itself was more than sound, so the RAF searched for a replacement powerplant and settled on the Rolls-Royce Merlin 61 as fitted to the Spitfire IX. Once mated with this battle-proven engine, the aircraft's performance was startling. Car builder Packard licence-built the Merlin as the V-1650, and North American followed the British lead in mating surplus P-51A airframes with the 'new' powerplant.

The Merlin-powered P-51B made its combat debut over Europe in December 1943, just when the USAAF's daylight bomber campaign had begun to falter. Here was its 'knight in shining armour', capable of escorting B-17s and B-24s on their hazardous missions. Over the next 19 months the Mustang became the dominant USAAF fighter across the globe. The RAF, too, got it's hands on more than 1,000 Merlin-powered aircraft through Lend-Lease. In total, 14,819 P-51s were built by North American. The fighter served on the frontline with the USAF into the early 1950s, and in Central and South America until the 1970s.

Mustang I AG470 of Flg Off H. Hills, No 414 Sqn RCAF,
Croydon, south London, August 1942

SPECIFICATIONS (P-51D)

Crew: Pilot

Length: 32ft 3in (9.83m)

Wingspan: 37ft (11.28m)

Height: 12ft 2in (3.71m)

Empty: 7,635lb (3,463kg)

Max T/O: 12,100lb (5,488kg)

Max Speed: 437mph (703km/h)

Range: 850 miles (1,368km)

Powerplant: Packard V-1650-7

Output: 1,720hp (1,283kW)

Armament: Six Browning 0.50in machine guns in wings; maximum bomb/rocket load of 1,000lb (454kg) on underwing racks

First Flight Date: 26 October 1940 (NA-73X)

P-51K-5 Mustang 44-11678 of Col I. Dregne, CO of the 357th FG, Leiston, Suffolk, April 1945

PLANE DETAILS

Previous page: The first victory claimed by a Mustang pilot – on 19 August 1942 – was appropriately made by an American, namely Flg Off Hollis Hills, who was serving with No 414 Sqn RCAF. He was flying this aircraft at the time, AG470 being adorned with a maple leaf badge. This was Hills' only victory with the RCAF, but he later transferred to the US Navy and became an ace flying F6F Hellcats in the Pacific. AG470 survived the war and was scrapped in 1947.

This page: A native of Viroqua, Wisconsin, Irwin Dregne commanded the 357th FG from 2 December 1944 until 21 July 1945, during which time he destroyed five enemy aircraft (two in the air and three on the ground) – the last two in this aircraft. The name *BOBBY JEANNE* referred to Dregne's wife and daughter, while *Ah Fung-Goo* was chosen by the crew chief. Dregne was an original member of the group, and he would eventually become its final wartime CO.

CURTISS SB2C HELLDIVER

The most numerous Allied dive-bomber of World War II, the Helldiver endured a prolonged gestation period to mature into one of the best aircraft of its type. The third Curtiss design to bear the appellation 'Helldiver', the aircraft had started life as the XSB2A-1 prototype. Built in response to a 1938 requirement issued by the US Navy for a new scout-bomber to replace the biplane SBC Helldiver, the aircraft showed such promise that large scale production was authorised a full 18 months before the first SB2C-1 left the Curtiss factory. Delays in its production were caused by the building of a new factory in Ohio and a USAAC order for 900 A-25As in April 1941. The latter machines were similar to the US Navy's SB2C-1, but embodied sufficient differences to further slow progress on the aircraft. Ironically, most A-25s were reassigned to the Marine Corps as SB2C-1As prior to reaching the USAAC.

Production Helldivers finally reached the US Navy in November 1942 when examples were issued to VS-9, but further delays in defining the aircraft's combat configuration prevented the Helldiver from making its service debut until November the following year, flying from USS *Bunker Hill*. At that time the SB2C-1 was still inferior in many respects to the Douglas SBD Dauntless – the aircraft it was meant to replace!

Some 7,200 were built between 1942–45, and despite being drastically improved during its service life (880 major design changes had to be made to the SB2C-1 before production could even get underway), the Helldiver retained an unenviable reputation, with more aircraft being lost in deck landing accidents than to enemy action. Indeed, its unpleasant flying characteristics near the stall earned it the nickname 'The Beast'. Although passionately disliked by many of the myriad crews sent into combat flying it, the Helldiver was responsible for the destruction of more Japanese targets than any other US dive-bomber. Post-war, the aircraft saw further use with the French, Italian, Greek and Portuguese navies and the Royal Thai Air Force, as well as with the US Navy Reserve.

SB2C-1C Helldiver BuNo 00334 'White 48' of VB-2, USS
Hornet (CV 12), central Pacific, June 1944

SPECIFICATIONS (SB2C-4)

Crew: Pilot and observer/gunner

Length: 36ft 8in (11.20m)

Wingspan: 49ft 9in (15.20m)

Height: 16ft 11in (5.10m)

Empty: 10,547lb (4,784kg)

Max T/O: 16,616lb (7,537kg)

Max Speed: 295mph (475km/h)

Range: 1,165 miles (1,875km)

Powerplant: Wright R-2600-20 Cyclone

Output: 1,900hp (1,417kW)

Armament: Two 20mm cannon or four Browning 0.50in machine guns in wings and two flexible Browning 0.30in machine guns in rear cockpit; maximum bomb/torpedo load of 1,000lb (454kg) in internal bomb-bay and 1,000lb (454kg) of bombs/rockets on underwing racks

First Flight Date: 18 December 1940

SB2C-5 Helldiver (BuNo unknown) 'White 82' of VB-10, USS *Intrepid* (CV 11), western Pacific, September 1945

PLANE DETAILS

Previous page: Assigned to Lt H. L. Buell, BuNo 00334 was a replacement aircraft that he flew only twice. The first time was from the escort carrier USS *Copahee* (CVE 12) to USS *Hornet* (CV 12) on 14 June, and the second, and last, time was six days later on the strike against the Japanese Mobile Fleet during the battle of the Philippine Sea. Buell led his division against the IJN aircraft carrier *Zuikaku*, and was wounded in the action. The Helldiver was written off when Buell crash-landed aboard USS *Lexington* (CV 16).

This page: 'Bombing 10' was one of the most experienced carrier squadrons in the US Navy by 1945. With two previous SBD cruises in USS *Enterprise* (CV 6) in 1942–43 and 1944, VB-10 exchanged its Dauntlesses for Helldivers in September 1944 and deployed aboard USS *Intrepid* (CV 11) in March 1945. Operations were conducted against Okinawa and Japan, but the vessel was forced back to the USA following a kamikaze attack on 16 April. VB-10 saw no further action in World War II.

GRUMMAN TBF/TBM AVENGER

Although Grumman was principally responsible for producing the majority of the US Navy's fighters during World War II, the company also designed and built the best carrier-based torpedo-bomber of the conflict in the shape of the TBF/TBM Avenger. Built as a replacement for the TBD Devastator, two prototype XTBF-1s were ordered from Grumman in April 1940. Completing its maiden flight on 1 August 1941, the prototype's portly appearance was due to its capacious internal bomb-bay, which was large enough to contain the biggest (22in) torpedo in the US Navy's arsenal. Powered by a Wright R-2600 Cyclone radial engine, the Avenger was also well-armed, with the pilot operating a forward-firing 0.50in machine gun, with a similar calibre weapon being fitted in the ventral position under the control of the bomb aimer and a 0.50in gun in a power-operated turret fired by the radio operator. Flight-testing proceeded rapidly, and by the end of January 1942 the first production TBF-1s were already being issued to the US Navy.

One of the astounding features of the Avenger story is that the basic design of the aircraft changed very little during the course of its production life. This allowed vast quantities to be built over a very short time scale – 2,293 were produced between January 1942 and December 1943 alone. The US Navy's demand for Avengers soon outstripped Grumman's production capacity, so General Motors (through the auspices of their Eastern Division) stepped into the breech and commenced production of the near identical TBM-1 from September 1942. By the time the Avenger production line closed in June 1945, GM had built 7,546 TBMs of various marks – a figure which far exceeded Grumman's own final build figure

More than 1,000 Avengers saw action with the Fleet Air Arm in both the Atlantic and the Pacific through to VJ Day, and two squadrons of RNZAF TBFs fought alongside American Avengers on Bougainville in 1944. The aircraft also served in the anti-submarine warfare and airborne early warning roles with the US Navy and foreign air arms well into the 1950s.

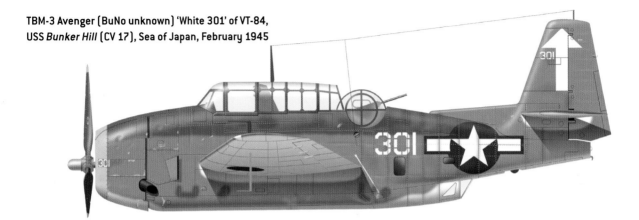

TBM-3 Avenger (BuNo unknown) 'White 301' of VT-84,
USS *Bunker Hill* (CV 17), Sea of Japan, February 1945

SPECIFICATIONS (TBM-3)

Crew: Pilot, bomb-aimer/gunner and radio operator/gunner

Length: 40ft (12.19m)

Wingspan: 54ft 2in (16.51m)

Height: 16ft 5in (5m)

Empty: 10,700lb (4,853kg)

Max T/O: 18,250lb (8,278kg)

Max Speed: 267mph (430km/h)

Range: 1,130 miles (1,819km)

Powerplant: Wright R-2600-20 Cyclone 14

Output: 1,750hp (1,305kW)

Armament: Two fixed Browning 0.50in machine guns in upper cowling and wing, as well as one in dorsal turret, and one Browning 0.30in machine gun in ventral position; maximum bomb/torpedo load of 2,000lb (907kg) in internal bomb-bay, as well as rockets/depth charges on underwing racks

First Flight Date: 1 August 1941

**Avenger I JZ159 of 852 Naval Air Squadron, HMS *Nabob*,
North Sea, early 1944**

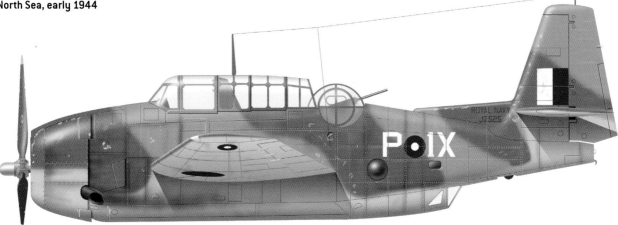

PLANE DETAILS

Previous page: This tri-colour TBM, marked with *Bunker Hill's* distinctive arrow 'G symbol', participated in the first carrier-launched strikes on Tokyo conducted by the Pacific Fleet in February 1945. Aircraft involved in this operation were marked with a yellow nose band as a special recognition symbol.

This page: Fleet Air Arm Avengers were initially called Tarpon Is until renamed Avengers on 12 January 1944. JZ159 saw considerable action with 852 NAS whilst embarked aboard the Canadian-manned escort carrier *Nabob* between 11 February and 6 April 1944, the aircraft flying anti-shipping strikes and parachute mine-laying sorties off the Norwegian coast.

VOUGHT F4U CORSAIR

Designed as a lightweight fighter built around the most powerful piston engine then available, Vought's prototype XF4U-1 was ordered by the US Navy in June 1938 following a study of the company's V-166 proposal. In order to harness the immense power of the Pratt & Whitney XR-2800 Double Wasp engine, the largest diameter propeller fitted to a fighter up to then had to be used by the prototype – sufficient ground clearance for the propeller was achieved through the use of an inverted gull wing. The future looked rosy for the aircraft, but modifications incorporated into the design as a result of lessons learned in combat over Europe left the Corsair unfit for carrier use. It was therefore left to the Marine Corps to give the aircraft its combat debut from Pacific island bases in February 1943, when VMF-124 made its first patrols from Guadalcanal in F4U-1 'birdcage' aircraft.

Just 688 framed canopy 'Dash-1s' were built before production switched to the more familiar 'bubble' canopy F4U-1A, this aircraft featuring a raised cockpit, strengthened landing gear and a small spoiler near the leading edge of the starboard wing to improve directional stability when the wheels touched the ground. All these modifications were deemed necessary to render the Corsair suitable for carrier use. Nevertheless, the US Navy remained hesitant about sending F4Us to sea until mid-1944, by which time the Royal Navy's Fleet Air Arm had been operating Corsairs from its carriers for more than six months. Ashore, a clutch of US Navy squadrons had been taking the fight to the Japanese, flying alongside similarly equipped Marine Corps units.

Aside from the 4,675 F4U-1A/C/Ds built by Vought, Brewster constructed 735 aircraft and Goodyear 4,014 (the latter designated FG-1s). The final production version of the Corsair built in World War II was the F4U-4, which featured a bigger engine and four-bladed propellers. The Corsair enjoyed a prosperous post-war career that lasted beyond the Korean War. Indeed, the final F4U-7 did not roll off the production line until 31 January 1952, it being the 12,571st, and last, Corsair built.

F4U-1 Corsair (BuNo unknown) 'White 17-F-13' of
Lt(jg) J. A. Halford, VF-17, USS Bunker Hill (CV 17),
north Atlantic, August 1943

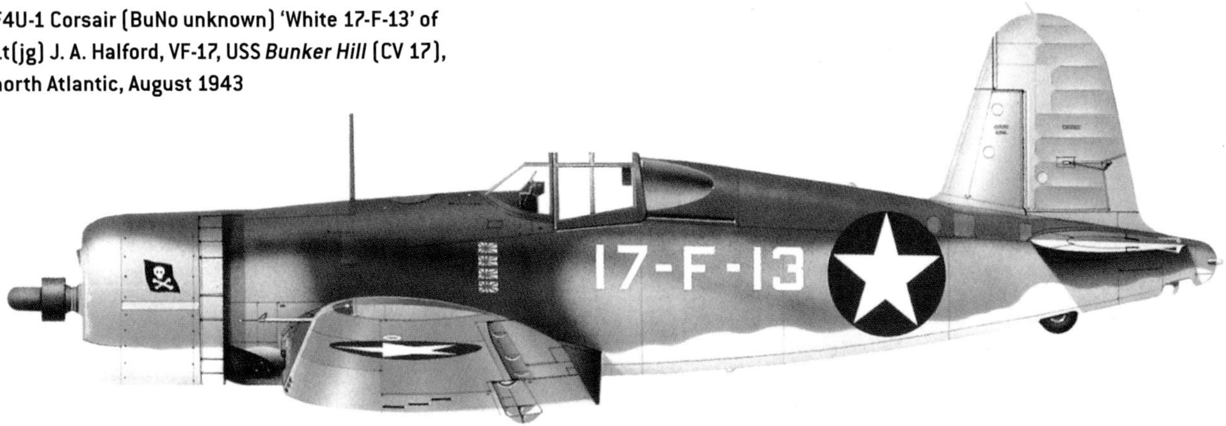

SPECIFICATIONS (F4U-4)

Crew: Pilot

Length: 33ft 8in (10.26m)

Wingspan: 40ft 11in (12.47m)

Height: 14ft 9in (4.50m)

Empty: 9,205lb (4,175kg)

Max T/O: 14,670lb (6,654kg)

Max Speed: 446mph (718km/h)

Range: 1,005 miles (1,617km)

Powerplant: Pratt & Whitney R-2800-18W
Double Wasp

Output: 2,450hp (1,827kW)

Armament: Six Browning 0.50in machine guns
in wings; provision for eight rockets under wings
or up to 2,000lb (907kg) bomb load under
fuselage centre section

First Flight Date: 29 May 1940

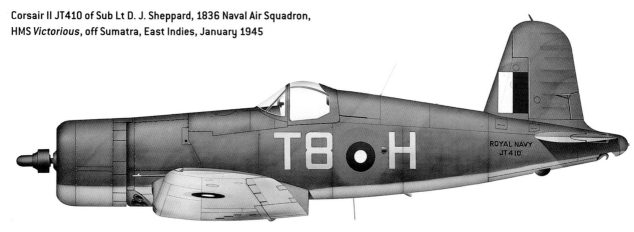

Corsair II JT410 of Sub Lt D. J. Sheppard, 1836 Naval Air Squadron, HMS *Victorious*, off Sumatra, East Indies, January 1945

ROYAL NAVY
JT410

PLANE DETAILS

Previous page: Looking resplendent in its newly applied three-tone camouflage scheme, finished off with early style national insignia, this aircraft was assigned to Lt(jg) James A. Halford. He had claimed four victories flying F4Fs over Guadalcanal in 1942, hence the victory symbols beneath the Corsair's cockpit. Halford was subsequently detached from VF-17 due to combat fatigue prior to claiming any further kills with the F4U.

This page: Canadian Corsair ace Don Sheppard claimed all five of his victories in this aircraft. The first two (Ki-43s) were scored during the Fleet Air Arm strike on Sumatran oil refineries on 4 January 1945. Sheppard downed a Ki-44 during the Palembang raid on 24 January, followed by two more 'Tojo' fighters shared with fellow ace Maj Ronnie Hay five days later. JT410 had also been used by another pilot to claim a Ki-43 kill over Car Nicobar the previous October.

AVRO LANCASTER

The RAF's most successful heavy bomber of World War II, the Lancaster was literally the 'phoenix that rose from the ashes' of the disastrous Manchester programme of 1940–41 to form the backbone of Bomber Command during the night bombing campaign against occupied Europe. The troublesome Manchester was powered by two Rolls-Royce Vultures, and boasted a layout near-identical to the Lancaster, but was plagued from the start by grave engine reliability problems. Avro realised that its airframe design was correct, however, and turned to Rolls-Royce and demanded access to the company's proven Merlin powerplant.

The Manchester had been chronically underpowered, so Avro's chief designer Roy Chadwick ensured that its replacement suffered no such problems by installing four Merlin Xs beneath the Lancaster's wing. The prototype (a converted Manchester airframe) first flew on 9 January 1941, an order for 1,070 bombers was placed with Avro just months later and the first production machines emerged that October. No 44 Sqn carried out the first operational sorties with the type in March 1942, and a further 58 Bomber Command units went on to see active service with the Lancaster, flying 156,000 sorties and dropping 608,612 tons of high explosive bombs and 51 million incendiaries. Aside from its exploits during the course of normal operations, the Lancaster is best known for the many special missions that it undertook, including the dams raid of May 1943 and the sinking of the battleship *Tirpitz* in November 1944.

Some 7,377 airframes were built by the six factories devoted to Lancaster production, this number being split between six distinctive marks. The B I and B III were similar apart from the installation of Packard Merlin engines in the latter, the B II was built with Hercules radial engines, the B VI had high-altitude Merlin 85s driving four-bladed propellers, the B VII was for service in the Far East and the B X was the Canadian-built version of the B III. Post-war, Lancasters survived in maritime patrol, transport and test trials roles until the late 1950s.

Lancaster B I R5570 of No 207 Sqn, Bottesford, Rutland, May 1942

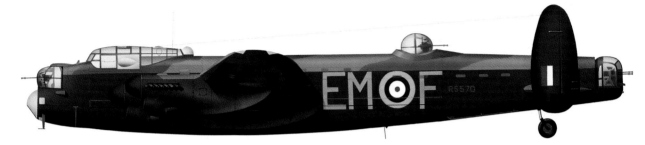

SPECIFICATIONS
(LANCASTER B I)

Crew: Pilot, flight engineer, navigator, bomb aimer/nose gunner, wireless operator, dorsal and tail turret gunners

Length: 69ft 6in (21.18m)

Wingspan: 102ft (31.09m)

Height: 20ft (6.10m)

Empty: 36,900lb (16,738kg)

Max T/O: 70,000lb (31,751kg)

Max Speed: 287mph (462km/h)

Range: 2,530 miles (4,072km)

Powerplant: four Rolls-Royce Merlin 24 engines

Output: 5,120hp (3,849.6kW)

Armament: Nose and dorsal turrets with two Browning 0.303in machine guns and tail turret with four Browning 0.303in machine guns; maximum bomb load of 14,000lb (6,350kg) in bomb-bay

First Flight Date: 9 January 1941

Lancaster B II LL725 of No 408 Sqn RCAF, Linton-on-Ouse, North Yorkshire, April 1944

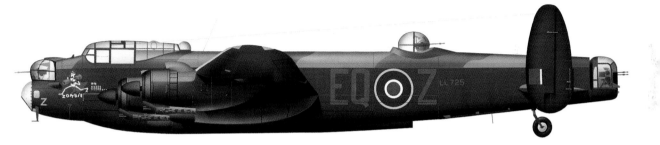

PLANE DETAILS

Previous page: Having initially been issued to No 83 Sqn, R5570 subsequently became one of the first B Is assigned to No 207 Sqn – the RAF's third Lancaster unit. A participant in each of Bomber Command's first two 'thousand bomber' raids at the end of May 1942, R5570 was lost on the 8/9 December mission to Turin whilst being flown by the unit CO, Wg Cdr F. G. L. Bain. The bomber had amassed 230 flying hours by the time it was shot down.

This page: Bearing a bomb log that included two swastikas for enemy aircraft shot down by its gunners, five bomb symbols indicating targets attacked in Germany and a row of maple leaves representing targets in the occupied countries of Europe, *ZOMBIE* failed to return from a mission to Hamburg on 29/30 July 1944.

LAVOCHKIN La-5/7

The LaGG-3 was the last of the new generation piston-engined fighters to enter service with the Red Air Force in early 1941, and from the start it earned an evil reputation from which it never recovered. Dubbed the 'Flying Coffin' due to its unique plastic-impregnated wooden construction and the ease with which it was shot down, the fighter's limited successes were gained at a high cost by stubborn and heroic pilots. Reports of the LaGG-3's inadequacies in combat resulted in the aircraft's inline M-105PF engine being replaced by the far more powerful Shvetsov M-82 radial in early 1942. Testing soon proved that the modified fighter was not only appreciably faster than its predecessor, but also far more capable at medium to high altitudes.

Designated the Lavochkin La-5, the first examples of the fighter to reach the frontline (during the battle for Stalingrad in late 1942) were actually re-engined LaGG-3s. Aside from the change of powerplant, the aircraft had also had its machine gun armament replaced by two 20mm cannon. By late March 1943 production of the definitive La-5N had commenced, this variant featuring a fuel-injected M-82FN for better performance at altitude, cut down rear fuselage decking and a new canopy for improved all round vision. The last single-seat fighter of wooden construction to see large-scale production and service, the La-5FN was more than a match for the Bf 109G and could hold its own with the Fw 190.

In November 1943 the further improved La-7 began trials, this model boasting even greater performance thanks to the lightening of its overall structure and adoption of the metal wing spars featured in late-build La-5FNs. Attention was also paid to reducing the fighter's drag coefficient, which resulted in the adoption of a revised cowling and inboard wing leading edge surfaces. The La-7 entered service in the spring of 1944, and went on to become the favoured mount of most Soviet aces. Further developments by Lavochkin resulted in the superlative La-9 and La-11, but these went into production too late to see service in the war.

La-5 'White 15' of Capt G. Kostylev, 4th GIAP-KBF,
Baltic Fleet, late summer 1943

SPECIFICATIONS (La-7)

Crew: Pilot

Length: 29ft 2.5in (8.90m)

Wingspan: 32ft 1.75in (9.80m)

Height: 8ft 6.25in (2.60m)

Empty: 5,842lb (2,620kg)

Max T/O: 7,496lb (3,400kg)

Max Speed: 423mph (680km/h)

Range: 615 miles (990km)

Powerplant: Shvetsov M-82FN

Output: 1,850hp (1,380kW)

Armament: Two or three 20mm cannon in upper cowling; provision for bombs or rockets under wings

First Flight Date: March 1942 (La-5)

La-7 'White 27' of Maj I. Kozhedub, 176th GIAP,
Germany, late April 1945

PLANE DETAILS

Previous page: Georgii Kostylev, a 46-victory ace, flew this La-5 after joining 4th GIAP-KBF in late August 1943. Aside from its dramatic 'snakesmouth', the fighter also boasts a Guards badge beneath the cockpit, which has had the standard banner titling *Gvardiia* (Guards) replaced with the word *Slava* (Glory).

This page: Ranking Soviet ace Ivan Kozhedub was issued with this La-7 in August 1944. The fighter arrived in the frontline with 48 kills and two Hero of the Soviet Union stars marked beneath the cockpit, but by the time Berlin fell the tally of victory stars had increased to 62. A third Hero star would also be added to the fighter on 18 August 1945. This aircraft has been exhibited in the Russian Air Force's Monino museum for many years.

BOEING B-29 SUPERFORTRESS

Boeing's timely response to the USAAC's request for a long-range strategic bomber to replace the B-17, the B-29 concept was devised soon after the Flying Fortress entered service in the late 1930s. Initially hindered by the lack of a suitable powerplant, the very long-range bomber project was resurrected in 1940 when five US manufacturers were invited to tender proposals. Eventually, only Consolidated and Boeing produced flyable prototypes, and although the former's XB-32 Dominator flew first, it was plagued by development problems. Boeing, however, was able to convince the USAAC that it could deliver production versions of its XB-29 by 1943, and the company duly won the contract for 1,500+ bombers *before* the prototype had even flown.

Boasting incredible advances in technology, including cabin pressurisation, tricycle landing gear, high wing loading and remote-controlled gun turrets, the first production B-29s were delivered in June 1943 to the 58th BW. The incredibly complex Superfortress suffered numerous technical problems in its first months of service, including in-flight fires with its 2,200hp Wright R-3350-23 Duplex Cyclone radial engines. However, by the time the four groups that made up the 58th BW moved to India in the spring of 1944, the B-29's reliability had improved.

The aircraft's first combat mission was flown on 5 June 1944, and within six months Superfortress operations were being mounted from newly built airfields in the Marianas Island chain in the western Pacific. Daily, 500 B-29s would be sent out to bomb targets in mainland Japan, these raids playing a crucial part in ending the conflict with the Japanese. The B-29 missions culminated with the two H-bomb strikes on Hiroshima and Nagasaki in August 1945. By the time production ceased in May 1946, 3,970 B-29s had been built. Post-war, the type enjoyed a long career in the USAF (including seeing considerable action in the Korean War), with 19 different variants performing numerous roles – including aerial refuelling, weather reconnaissance and mother ship for supersonic research aircraft – into the early 1960s.

B-29-60-BW Superfortress 44-69736 of the 39th BS/6th BG, North Field, Tinian, June 1945

SPECIFICATIONS (B-29)

Crew: Pilot and co-pilot, flight engineer, navigator, bombardier/nose gunner, radar operator, radio operator, central fire controller/top gunner, right and left gunners and tail gunner

Length: 99ft (30.18m)

Wingspan: 141ft 3in (43.05m)

Height: 29ft 7in (9.02m)

Empty: 70,140lb (31,815kg)

Max T/0: 124,000lb (56,245kg)

Max Speed: 358mph (576km/h)

Range: 3,250 miles (5,230km)

Powerplant: four Wright R-3350-23 Duplex Cyclones

Output: 8,800hp (6,564kW)

Armament: Four turrets with four Browning 0.50in machine guns on top/bottom of fuselage and tail turret with 20mm cannon and two Browning 0.50in machine guns; 20,000lb (9,072kg) of bombs in bomb-bay

First Flight Date: 21 September 1942

B-29-55-MO Superfortress 44-86415 of the 343rd BS/98th BG, Yokota, Japan, September 1951

PLANE DETAILS

Previous page: Marked up in 6th BG markings, which featured a 313th Bomb Wing circle containing the group letter 'R', as well as the group colour red on both the tail tip and the engines' upper nacelles, 44-69736 survived the war. When the bomber's crew attempted to ferry the B-29 back to the US, the aircraft suffered four successive engine failures that resulted in the Superfortress being abandoned on Kwajalein Atoll in the Marshall Islands. It was eventually destroyed there during fire training in mid-1946.

This page: This B-29 was one of a number of Superfortresses whose undersides were sprayed with jet black paint so as to make the aircraft less easy to spot when targeted by North Korean flak battery crews. 44-86415 was lost when it ditched into the Sea of Japan during a leaflet dropping mission on 19 September 1951. None of its crew were recovered despite a search and rescue operation being promptly mounted.

GRUMMAN F6F HELLCAT

The Hellcat was always destined to be a success, as it embodied the early lessons learnt by users of Grumman's previous fleet fighter, the F4F Wildcat, in the Pacific, as well as general pointers from the RAF's experience in Europe. The original design for the Hellcat dated back to late 1940, and the US Navy placed an advance order for the fighter in June 1941. Modifications to the 'paper' aircraft in light of combat experience from the Battle of the Coral Sea in May 1942 saw Grumman lower the wing centre section to enable the undercarriage to be wider splayed, the fitment of more armour-plating around the cockpit to protect the pilot and an increase in the fighter's ammunition capacity for its six 0.50in machine guns.

Less than a year after the US Navy placed its order, the prototype XF6F-1 made its first flight. Grumman soon realised that a more powerful engine was needed to give the fighter a combat edge, so a Pratt & Whitney R-2800-10 was installed, resulting in the F-1 being redesignated F-3. Rushed into production following successful testing of the re-engined prototype, the F6F-3 first saw action with VF-5 aboard USS *Yorktown* (CV 10) in August 1943. The Hellcat served aboard most fleet carriers in varying numbers, and was credited with the destruction of 4,947 aircraft up to VJ Day. All the leading US Navy aces of the war flew Hellcats, with the premier fighter squadron in the Pacific, VF-15, downing 310 enemy aircraft with the rugged Grumman.

Amazingly, only three major variants of the F6F were produced – the -3, of which 4,423 were constructed between October 1942 and April 1944, the improved -5 day fighter and the specialised -3N and -5N nightfighters. By the time the last Hellcat was delivered in November 1945, 12,275 had been built. The Royal Navy's Fleet Air Arm was also a great believer in the Hellcat, procuring almost 1,200 between 1943–45. Post-war, the aircraft saw extensive service with the US Naval Reserve and training units, whilst surplus Hellcats were converted into pilotless F6F-3/5K target drones for missile testing.

F6F-5 Hellcat BuNo 58937/'White 12' of Lt(jg) R. 'Hawk' Hawkins, VF-31, USS *Cabot* (CVL 28), western Pacific, September 1944

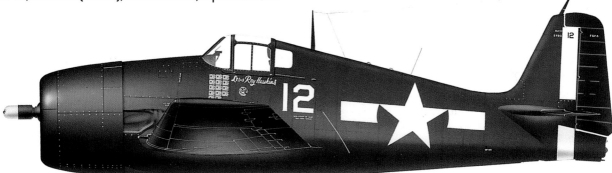

SPECIFICATIONS (F6F-5)

Crew: Pilot

Length: 33ft 7in (10.24m)

Wingspan: 42ft 10in (13.06m)

Height: 13ft 6in (4.11m)

Empty: 9,153lb (4,152kg)

Max T/O: 15,413lb (6,991kg)

Max Speed: 380mph (612km/h)

Range: 945 miles (1,512km)

Powerplant: Pratt & Whitney R-2800-10W Double Wasp

Output: 2,000hp (1,491kW)

Armament: Six Browning 0.50in machine guns in wings; provision for six rockets under wings or up to 2,000lb (907kg) of bombs under centre section

First Flight Date: 26 June 1942

Hellcat I JV125 of Lt Cdr S. G. Orr, CO of 804 Naval Air Squadron, HMS _Emperor_, North Sea, May 1944

PLANE DETAILS

Previous page: This aircraft was flown by Texan 'Hawk' Hawkins, who was the second-ranking ace of VF-31 'Flying Meataxes' with 14 kills – five of these (Ki-43s) were claimed in this fighter on 13 September 1944. VF-31 was assigned a mixed fleet of 14 F6F-3s and 10 F6F-5s during its 1944 Pacific deployment.

This page: On 14 May 1944 Hellcats from _Emperor_'s 800 and 804 NASs, led by Lt Cdr Orr in this aircraft, were on an anti-shipping strike off the Norwegian coast when they spotted five He 115 seaplanes off Rorvik. Aces Orr and Lt Ritchie jointly shot one down, the latter pilot having already despatched a He 115. The remaining three seaplanes alighted on the water, where they were sunk by the strafing Hellcats. These proved to be the last Luftwaffe victories claimed by Fleet Air Arm Hellcats.

MESSERSCHMITT Me 262

The world's very first operational jet fighter, the Me 262 was also the most advanced aircraft of its generation to actually see combat. Design work on the Messerschmitt commenced as early as 1938, and the first tailwheeled prototype, fitted with a nose-mounted Junkers Jumo 210 piston engine, completed its maiden flight on 4 April 1941. Unfortunately for Messerschmitt, work on the aircraft's revolutionary turbojet powerplants failed to keep pace with its development of the airframe, and it was not until 18 July 1942 that the first successful flight was made with the preferred Junkers Jumo 003 turbojets installed – the BMW 003 had initially been trialled, but persistent failures had seen it discarded in early 1942.

With the engine/airframe combination at last sorted out, political interference from no less a figure than the Führer himself saw the programme side-tracked for a number of months as he insisted that the aircraft be developed as a bomber. Sense finally prevailed in early 1944, and the first aircraft to reach the frontline saw combat in June of that year. In the vanguard of a new crop of 'wonder weapons' that were issued to the Luftwaffe from mid-1944, the Me 262 was far in advance of anything the Allies had even in the experimental phase. This in turn meant the fighter could perform its mission with relative impunity.

Despite Germany being bombed virtually 24 hours a day during the final 12 months of the war, more than 1,400 Me 262s were completed by Messerschmitt, and a further 500 were lost in air raids. Engine reliability, fuel shortages and unrealistic operational taskings restricted the frontline force to around 200 jets at any one time, but these nevertheless accounted for more than 200 Allied aircraft (*Jagdwaffe* claims exceeded 745 victories for the Me 262!) during day and night interceptions. Flying with eight units, including *Jagdgeschwader* 7, *Jagdverband* 44, *Nachtjagdgeschwader* 11 and *Ergänzungs-jagdgeschwader* 2, some 28 pilots 'made ace' flying the jet with the seven units that saw combat.

Me 262A-1a Wk-Nr 501221 of Oberfeldwebel H. Buchner, III./JG 7, Prague-Ruzyn,
Czechoslovakia, April 1945

SPECIFICATIONS
(Me 262A-1AI.C.)

Crew: Pilot

Length: 34ft 9.5in (10.60m)

Wingspan: 41ft 0.5in (12.51m)

Height: 11ft 6.75in (3.83m)

Empty: 9,742lb (4,420kg)

Max T/O: 14,101lb (6,396kg)

Max Speed: 540mph (870km/h)

Range: 652 miles (1,050km)

Powerplants: two Junkers Jumo 004B-1/-2 or -3 turbojet engines

Output: 3,960lb st (17.8kN)

Armament: Four 30mm cannon in nose and provision for 24 underwing rockets

First Flight Date: 18 July 1942 (first all jet-powered flight)

Me 262B-1a/U1 Wk-Nr 111980 of Ltn H. Altner, 10./NJG 11, Reinfeld, Germany, May 1945

PLANE DETAILS

Previous page: Flown by 46-victory ace Hermann Buchner, this aircraft fell foul of US light anti-aircraft fire while its pilot was carrying out a low-level strafing sweep south of Salzwedel, in Saxony, on 21 April 1945. Buchner made a successful wheels-up landing near Klötze and was captured, while the carcass of 'Yellow 3' remained in the field that it had crashed in for many months, a magnet for souvenir-hungry US occupation troops.

This page: One of seven interim nightfighters delivered to 10./NJG 11 during the unit's brief operational career, this aircraft was fitted with FuG 218 Neptun V radar and two 300-litre drop tanks on the ETC 503 weapons rack under the nose. Surrendered to British forces at Schleswig-Jagel, 'Red 12' was transported back to the UK for evaluation post-war. It was finally scrapped in 1948 after being damaged in a violent storm the previous winter.

YAKOVLEV Yak-3

Yakovlev were responsible for producing the most successful series of fighter aircraft used by the USSR during World War II, starting with the Yak-1. The second aircraft from this design bureau to be designated the Yak-3 (the first was abandoned in 1941 due to poor engine reliability and a shortage of suitable building materials), this machine was built to fulfil a Red Air Force requirement for an agile fighter capable of achieving its maximum performance at low altitude. By meeting these criteria, the aircraft bestowed upon the Red Air Force the ability to maintain air superiority over the battlefield – something that the Luftwaffe had enjoyed for much of the war on the Eastern Front.

Utilising a modified Yak-1M fitted with a smaller wing, the prototypes completed their service trials on October 1943, by which time a small pre-series run of aircraft had been put into production at GAZ 286 at Kamensk Ural'ski. The Yak-3 was not cleared for production until June 1944, and the small number of regiments that rapidly re-equipped with the fighter soon proved the fighter's superiority over its Luftwaffe counterparts in a number of aerial engagements – it was so dominant in combat that the Luftwaffe ordered that its fighter pilots avoid intercepting Yaks encountered below 16,400ft (5,000m). The Yak-3 proved to be exceptionally manoeuvrable, with only modest pressure on the control column producing fast and accurate snap rolls. The fighter's stalling speed was high, however, and it had an alarming tendency to drop a wing on approach to landing unless the pilot kept the speed up.

In the autumn of 1943 Yakovlev replaced the 1,300hp Klimov M-105PF engine in the Yak-3 with a 1,650hp M-107A to create the Yak-3U, the latter machine going into production in early 1945 – too late for the Yak-3U to achieve operational deployment in World War II. This version also saw the Yak fighter's traditional mixed structure replaced with light alloy skinning. Production of the definitive Yak-3U would continue until early 1946, by which time 4,848 examples of all types had been built.

Yak-3 of Lt Savelii Vasil'evich Nosov, 150th GIAP,
Czechoslovakia, early 1945

SPECIFICATIONS (Yak-3)

Crew: Pilot

Length: 27ft 10.25in (8.49m)

Wingspan: 30ft 2.25in (9.20m)

Height: 7ft 11.25in (2.42m)

Empty: 4,641lb (2,105kg)

Max T/O: 5,864lb (2,660kg)

Max Speed: 407mph (655km/h)

Range: 559 miles (900km)

Powerplant: Klimov M-105PF

Output: 1,650hp (1,230kW)

Armament: One 20mm cannon in propeller hub
and two 12.7mm machine guns in upper cowling

First Flight Date: Late 1942

Yak-3 of Maj Gen Georgii Nefyodovich Zakharov, Commander 303rd IAD, East Prussia, early 1945

PLANE DETAILS

Previous page: Nosov arrived at the front in June 1943 and was selected for 4th IAK's special hunter squadron, whose members painted the noses of their fighters blood red. By the end of the war Nosov had flown 149 sorties and scored 16 individual and one shared victories in 38 combats. He became a Hero of the Soviet Union on 15 May 1946.

This page: This aircraft displays the standard dark and light grey camouflage of the period, as well as 303rd IAD's lightning bolt insignia, the Order of the Red Banner on the nose and Zakharov's personal crest. The insignia honours one of Russia's most famous icons, St George the Victory-Bearer patron saint of Moscow, Russia and, in particular, the Russian Army pre-1918. A man who led from the front despite his high rank, Zakharov completed 153 sorties and claimed ten victories to add to his 11 kills pre-war in Spain and China.

MIKOYAN MiG-15

As the first truly successful Soviet jet fighter, the MiG-15 arrived virtually unannounced in the skies over war-torn Korea in 1950 and provided United Nations' pilots with a rather unpleasant shock. With its all-swept wing and aerodynamic design, the MiG could easily out-climb, out-dive, out-manoeuvre and out-pace its US and British jet contemporaries, and it was only with the hasty arrival of the F-86A Sabre in December 1950 that UN forces could at last field a type that was capable of matching the MiG-15 in most areas. Aircraft from 151st GvIAD were the first to see combat, and clashes with US fighters in particular would become an everyday part of the war until the conflict ended in July 1953 – by which time ten Soviet fighter divisions had fought with UN aircraft in the skies over North Korea.

At the 'heart' of the nimble fighter from the Mikoyan-Gurevich bureau was the compact Klimov RD-45F turbojet engine, which was a direct descendent of the Rolls-Royce Nene. Examples of the latter powerplant had been sent to the USSR in 1947 by a then-friendly British government, and these proved to be the answer to the engine problem that had up until that point stalled Soviet jet fighter development. The Mikoan-Gurevich bureau designers were also heavily influenced by German data captured during the final days of World War II.

Following flight-testing in early 1948, the MiG-15 was placed into series production, and within five years 8,000 had been built in the USSR. Further improved variants (including the two-seat UTI trainer) were ushered into service during the 1950s, with licence production continuing in Poland (Lim-1 fighter and SBLim-2 two-seater) and Czechoslovakia (as the S-103 – these were the best built in the world) into the early 1960s. Most fighters were built to MiG-15bis specification, being fitted with a more powerful VK-1A engine, perforated flaps and redesigned rear-fuselage airbrakes. The fighter variant remained in frontline service with a number of air forces into the 1970s, while the last examples of the two-seat UTI trainer were not retired until the 1990s.

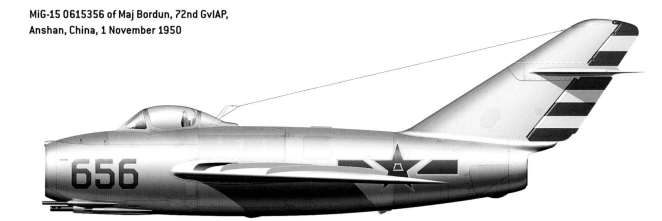

MiG-15 0615356 of Maj Bordun, 72nd GvIAP,
Anshan, China, 1 November 1950

SPECIFICATIONS (MiG-15)

Crew: Pilot

Length: 35ft 7.50in (10.86m)

Wingspan: 33ft 1in (10.08m)

Height: 12ft 1.7in (3.70m)

Empty: 8,115lb (3,681kg)

Max T/O: 11,861lb (5,380kg)

Max Speed: 667mph (1,076km/h)

Range: 826 miles (1,330km)

Powerplant: Klimov VK-1

Output: 5,952lb st (26.4kN)

Armament: One N-37 37mm cannon and
two NS-23 23mm cannon in nose

First Flight Date: 20 December 1947

MiG-15bis 2915316 of Maj S. A. Fedorets, 913th IAP,
Antung, China, July 1953

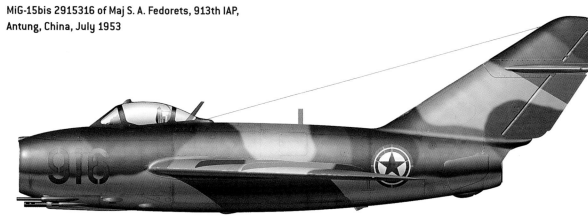

PLANE DETAILS

Previous page: Built by Factory No 153 at Novosibirsk, this aircraft was flown by 2nd Squadron CO Maj Bordun on 1 November 1950, when he led a group of 72nd GvIAP aircraft in the first ever jet-versus-jet dogfight. Soviet pilots claimed a kill during the clash with USAF F-80 Shooting Stars. This MiG-15 was eventually passed on to the Chinese-manned 9th IAP, 3rd IAD in late January 1951.

This page: Semyon Fedorets scored two victories while flying MiG-15bis 2915316, which was built by Factory No 153 in 1952. Assigned to the ace between May and July 1953, the fighter was handed over to 37th IAD the following month. During its time with the latter division, the jet was fitted with an ASP-4N gunsight and an SRD-1 radar range finder. 64th IAK transferred it to a 54th Air Army unit in November 1954.

NORTH AMERICAN F-86 SABRE

Aside from the Bell UH-1 Huey, no other post-war Western combat aircraft has been built in as great a number as the F-86. Total production, including licence-built examples in Canada, Australia and Japan, amounted to 9,502 airframes with no fewer than 13 separate land- and sea-based variants. The first contracts for the fighter were placed by the USAAF and US Navy in 1944, although the initial design featured unswept wings and a fuselage of greater diameter to allow it to house the Allison J35-2 engine. Following examination of captured German jet aircraft and related documentation, North American altered the fighter's shape, although the US Navy still received 30 FJ-1 Furies, featuring the original wing, fuselage and powerplant.

The revised XP-86, however, was a vastly superior machine, featuring wings with a 35-degree sweep angle, a lengthened fuselage, pressurised cockpit, power-boosted ailerons and automatic leading edge slots. The XP-86 made its maiden flight on 1 October 1947, and the USAF ordered 221 Sabres two months later. These began reaching squadrons in February 1949, and several US-based wings had swapped their F-80s for F-86As by the time the Sabre was committed to combat in Korea in December 1950. Going head-to-head with the equally impressive Soviet-built MiG-15, the F-86 soon proved its superiority during numerous dogfights with the communist fighter. Combat duly ushered in further improvements to the aircraft, with the F-86E (393 built between 1950–52) featuring an all-flying tail to boost the jet's manoeuvrability at high speeds. The definitive Korean War era Sabre was the F-86F, which was fitted with a revised profile wing that improved the jets handling at high altitude.

Post-war, the radar-equipped F-86D enjoyed widespread use with Air Defense Command as its first all-weather interceptor. A dynasty of US Navy fighters in the form of the FJ-2/3 and -4 also served the fleet well into the late 1950s. Examples of the F-86 remained in the active inventory of a number of air forces into the early 1990s.

F-86A-5 Sabre 49-1109 of Capt R. D. Gibson, 335th FS/4th FW, Suwon, South Korea, September 1951

SPECIFICATIONS (F-86A)

Crew: Pilot

Length: 37ft 6.50in (11.44m)

Wingspan: 37ft 1.50in (11.32m)

Height: 14ft 8in (4.47m)

Empty: 10,093lb (4,578kg)

Max T/O: 16,223lb (7,359kg)

Max Speed: 679mph (1,093km/h)

Range: 660 miles (1,060km)

Powerplant: General Electric J47-GE-13

Output: 5,200lb st (22kN)

Armament: Six Browning M-2 0.50in machine guns in nose; maximum bomb/rocket load of 2,000lb (907kg) on two underwing stores pylons

First Flight Date: 1 October 1947 (XP-86)

F-86F-1 Sabre 51-2897 of 2Lt J. L. Thompson,
39th FS/51st FW, Suwon, South Korea, July 1953

PLANE DETAILS

Previous page: Ralph Gibson became the USAF's third jet ace while flying missions in this Sabre between May and September 1951. The fighter was also used by fellow ace 1Lt Richard Becker to claim his first two MiG-15 kills (on 22 April and 8 July 1951). Shortly after Gibson completed his tour, 49-1109 was shot down by a MiG-15 on 24 October 1951 and its pilot captured.

This page: Arguably the most garish Sabre to see combat in Korea, this jet was assigned to the 39th FS in the autumn of 1952. Having been flown by several other pilots, it was allocated to 2Lt Thompson in the spring of 1953. He used the fighter to claim two MiG-15 kills, one of which was decorated with a dragon motif. This inspired the Sabre's crew chief to apply one to 51-2897 as well. Surviving the conflict, the F-86 was supplied to the Chinese Nationalist Air Force in late 1954.

GRUMMAN F9F PANTHER

As Grumman's first jet fighter, the F9F was originally designed to be powered by four small axial-flow Westinghouse 19XB (J30) jet engines. However, the US Navy had been monitoring the performance of the Rolls-Royce Nene, and duly had two examples shipped to the Naval Air Test Center in Philadelphia for testing. The engine's performance was so revelatory that it was soon placed in licence-production by Pratt & Whitney as the J42. The prototype XF9F-1 Panther made use of one of the 'imports' to complete its flight trials in 1947–48.

A conventional design with straight wings and excellent low speed handling for carrier operations, the first of 567 F9F-2s reached fleet squadron VF-51 in May 1949. Unlike the prototypes, all production aircraft had permanent wingtip tanks fitted. Following the interim 'Dash-3' and '-4', Grumman commenced production of the definitive F9F-5 (725 built, including 109 modified F9F-4s) in late 1950, this variant introducing a longer fuselage, taller tail and more powerful J48 turbojet. These modifications went some way to improving the Panther's poor straightline speed, although this problem was not totally addressed until the advent of the swept-wing F9F-6 Cougar in 1951.

The first carrier-based jet to see action over Korea on 6 August 1950, the Panther performed almost half the attack missions flown during the war by US Navy and Marine Corps units – no fewer than 24 squadrons equipped with F9Fs were committed to the conflict. Although principally used as an attack jet, the Panther was also a successful photo-reconnaissance platform, with oblique and vertical cameras fitted in the lengthened nose section of the F9F-2/5P. These aircraft also saw extensive use over Korea throughout the war. Following their replacement in the fleet by swept-wing Cougars and Furies soon after the Korean War had ended in July 1953, surviving Panthers were converted into pilotless target drones (F9F-2/5KD), or manned drone controllers. The handful of surviving F9F-5KDs were redesignated DF-9Es in 1962.

F9F-2 Panther (BuNo unknown) of Lt L. Plog, VF-51, USS
Valley Forge (CV 45), Sea of Japan, July 1950

SPECIFICATIONS (F9F-5)

Crew: Pilot

Length: 35ft 10in (10.69m)

Wingspan: 38ft (11.58m)

Height: 12ft 3in (3.74m)

Empty: 10,147lb (4,603kg)

Max T/O: 18,721lb (8,492kg)

Max Speed: 579mph (926km/h)

Range: 1,300 miles (2,080km)

Powerplant: Pratt & Whitney J42-P-6A

Output: 6,250lb st (30kN)

Armament: Four M-2 20mm cannon in nose; provision for up to 2,000lb (907kg) of bombs/rockets on six underwing stores pylons

First Flight Date: 24 November 1947

F9F-5 Panther (BuNo unknown) of Lt(jg) J. D. Middleton, VF-781,
USS *Oriskany* (CV-34), Sea of Japan, November 1952

PLANE DETAILS

Previous page: On 3 July 1950, this aircraft was one of eight F9F-2s from VF-51 'Screaming Eagles' that launched from CV 45 to escort a strike mission targeting Pyongyang airfield. It was the first combat sortie ever made by jet-powered US Navy aircraft, and in the ensuing melée over the North Korean airfield Ens E. W. Brown and Lt(jg) Leonard Plog each shot down a communist Yak-9 fighter. Two other VF-51 pilots destroyed Yaks on the ground.

This page: After an unusual aerial clash on 18 November 1952 involving three F9F-5s and as many as eight MiG-15s, Middleton and his wingman Lt E. R. Williams were credited with two victories. This incident was initially hushed up by the US Navy, as the enemy aircraft had been identified as Russian MiG-15s (not North Korean ones) operating from a base near Vladivostok. Williams and Middleton were both awarded the Silver Star for their aerial success.

MARTIN B-57 CANBERRA

When the USAF selected the English Electric Canberra to serve as a tactical attack bomber in the late 1940s, it was the first time a foreign combat aircraft had been chosen for frontline service with the US military in large numbers since 1918. Martin was given the contract to manufacture the British jet under licence, the moderately Americanised B-57A entering service in July 1953, with the bulk of the 75 built being re-rolled as RB-57 photo-reconnaissance platforms upon delivery.

Martin heavily modified the follow-on B-57B in order to make it a more adaptable attack aircraft, particularly at low level. Featuring a fighter-style canopy and no nose glazing, the jet had additional underwing pylons, a rotary bomb-bay door (originally developed by Martin for its unsuccessful XB-51 tri-jet bomber) and improved avionics. A total of 202 B-57Bs were built, followed by 38 B-57C trainers, 20 RB-57D high altitude reconnaissance platforms and 68 B-57E target tugs.

While not receiving as much publicity as the F-105 and F-4 fighter-bombers, which took the fight into the heart of North Vietnam, the B-57 was nevertheless the first jet-powered US attack aircraft committed to this conflict. It was involved in day-to-day interdiction missions against traffic coming down the Ho Chi Minh Trail, shooting up trucks and bombing and strafing sampans in the Mekong Delta. The aircraft also flew classified 'black' missions over the border into Laos and Cambodia. The B-57B hit targets in North and South Vietnam between 1965 and 1969, while later in the war many aircraft were upgraded to the then-state-of-the-art B-57G night intruder, which became one of the most valuable weapons in the USAF inventory. Fitted with target sensors that permitted all-weather operations with precision-guided weapons, G-model Canberras proved particularly effective in the latter stages of the conflict. Although most surviving B-57s had been retired by the mid-1970s, a small number of specialist electronic warfare (RB-57), weather reconnaissance (WB-57) and target tug (EB-57) variants served with the Air National Guard until 1982.

B-57B 53-3925 Canberra of the 13th BS/405th TFW ADVON 1,
Tan Son Nhut AB, South Vietnam, June 1965

SPECIFICATIONS (B-57B)

Crew: Pilot and navigator

Length: 65ft 6in (19.96m)

Wingspan: 64ft (19.50m)

Height: 15ft 7in (4.75m)

Empty: 26,800lb (12,200kg)

Max T/O: 55,000lb (24,950kg)

Max Speed: 582mph (937km/h)

Range: 2,100 miles (3,380km)

Powerplant: two Wright J65-5s

Output: 14,440lb st (33kN)

Armament: Provision for four 20mm cannon or eight 0.50in machine guns in outer wings; bomb-bay load of 5,000lb (2,268kg), plus rockets/bombs on eight underwing and two wingtip stores pylons

First Flight Date: 20 July 1953

B-57G 53-3931 Canberra of the 13th BS/8th TFW,
Ubon RTAB, Thailand, December 1970

PLANE DETAILS

Previous page: This aircraft arrived at Clark AB, in the Philippines, destined for Vietnam, on 11 May 1965. 53-3925 flew missions from Tan Son Nhut Air Base (AB) until it moved with its unit to Da Nang AB some two months later. This aircraft is armed with 750lb M117 general purpose bombs beneath its wings. 53-3925 was lost on 14 April 1966 when it collided with sister-aircraft 53-3926 during a practice formation flight over Da Nang. Both jets were assigned to the 8th BS, and all four crewmen survived the accident.

This page: This former B-57B was one of the first USAF Canberras deployed to Vietnam, arriving at Bien Hoa in September 1964 with the 8th BS. Like all B-57Gs, it carries first-generation 500lb laser-guided bombs on its four underwing pylons. This aircraft had the unhappy distinction of being the only B-57G lost in combat when it collided with an O-2A forward air control aircraft on the night of 12 December 1970. The Canberra crew survived but the FACs in the Cessna did not.

NORTH AMERICAN F-100 SUPER SABRE

The natural successor to the F-86, the F-100 Super Sabre was larger and more powerful than its famous forebear. It was also capable of breaking the sound barrier in level flight, which was a first for any combat aircraft. Development on the F-100 had commenced as early as February 1949, and the overall size and shape of the fighter was barely influenced by air combat over Korea. Indeed, had lessons from that conflict been incorporated into the aircraft, it would have been a less complex design with the best possible rate of climb and performance at high altitude. Known as the Model 180, the aircraft adhered to the F-86's configuration to the point where it was initially called the Sabre 45 due to the angle of wing sweepback.

In November 1951 the USAF ordered two prototypes and 110 production aircraft, which it designated F-100A Super Sabres. The prototype YF-100 made its first flight on 25 May 1953, and flight-testing progressed so rapidly that production F-100As (203 built up to March 1954) started leaving North American's Inglewood plant just five months later. Although the 479th TFW was declared operational in September 1954, a series of flight control-related crashes saw the F-100A grounded two months later. North American quickly rectified these problems by lengthening both the jet's wings and vertical fin, and the Super Sabre's handling was never an issue again.

Production switched to the F-100C fighter-bomber in September 1955, and a staggering 476 examples were built for the USAF in less than 18 months. The definitive F-100D followed, this variant having an enlarged fin/rudder and additional underwing pylons. No fewer than 1,264 D-models were built, and more than 500 of these were written off in crashes from mid-1956 through to the mid-1970s. North American also built 339 F-100F two-seaters between March 1957 and October 1959. F-100C/D/Fs saw action in Vietnam, with four fighter wings being based in-theatre. The Air National Guard also received plenty of F-100s, with 23 units flying them from 1958 through to 1979. Super Sabres were also flown by France, Denmark, Turkey and Taiwan.

F-100F-10-NA Super Sabre 56-3868 of the 522nd TFS/27th TFW,
Clark AB, the Philippines, November 1965

SPECIFICATIONS (F-100D)

Crew: Pilot

Length: 49ft 6in (15.09m)

Wingspan: 38ft 9.50in (11.81m)

Height: 16ft 2.75in (4.96m)

Empty: 21,000lb (9,525kg)

Max T/O: 34,832lb (15,800kg)

Max Speed: 864mph (1,390km/h)

Range: 1,500 miles (2,415km)

Powerplant: Pratt & Whitney J57-PW-39

Output: 16,950lb st (75kN)

Armament: Four M-39E 20mm cannon in nose; maximum bomb/rocket/missile load of 7,500lb (3,402kg) on six underwing stores pylons

First Flight Date: 25 May 1953

F-100D-91-NA Super Sabre 56-3233 of the 306th TFS/31st TFW, Tuy Hoa AB, South Vietnam, 1969

PLANE DETAILS

Previous page: 56-3868 flew with the 27th TFW in Vietnam. It subsequently served with the 4th, followed by the 37th, 35th, 474th and 31st TFWs. The 27th TFW performed the last regular USAF F-100 sortie on 19 July 1972. This F-100F then flew with Connecticut, Georgia and Missouri Air National Guard (ANG) units before withdrawal to the Military Aircraft Storage and Disposition Center at Davis-Monthan AFB, in Arizona, on 3 January 1979 and eventual conversion into a QF-100F target drone.

This page: This aircraft spent its first eight years with the US Air Forces in Europe (USAFE), assigned to the 50th TFW at Toul-Rosieres AB, in France, and Hahn AB, in West Germany, prior to joining the 31st TFW in August 1966 and seeing combat in Vietnam. 56-3233 then flew with the Ohio and Missouri ANGs before conversion into a full-scale aerial target and subsequent destruction in March 1987.

BOEING B-52 STRATOFORTRESS

For many years the biggest, heaviest and most powerful bomber ever built, the B-52 may have been eclipsed by the Tu-160 in terms of offensive potential, but it is likely to remain a viable frontline weapon of war long after the Tupolev bomber has been consigned to history. Originally planned by Boeing in 1946 as a B-50 Washington replacement, the aircraft was to have been a straight-winged bomber that relied on turboprop engines due to the lack of available powerplants capable of propelling an intercontinental bomber. However, the B-52 became a direct beneficiary of Pratt & Whitney's fuel-efficient J57 turbojet, which was far superior to its rivals in terms of performance and economy.

Redesigned with eight engines housed in four double pods beneath swept wings, the prototype YB-52 completed its first flight on 15 April 1952. Initially built with tandem seating for the pilot and co-pilot, production B-52As had a revised side-by-side layout in an airliner style cockpit. Re-equipping B-50 squadrons from March 1955, the B-52 was produced to the tune of 744 airframes in eight sub-types. Numerically, the most important of these was the B-52D (170), which played a key role in the Vietnam War and was the backbone of Strategic Air Command's Cold War nuclear bomber force into the 1970s, and the B-52G (193 built), with its smaller fin and remote-controlled tail guns.

The final production variant was the B-52H (102 built), which was similar to the G-model except for its eight Pratt & Whitney TF33 turbofan engines and 20mm cannon in the tail turret, rather than four 0.50in machine guns. The B-52G saw extensive combat in Operation *Desert Storm* in 1991, as it was capable of employing conventional cruise missiles and iron bombs. The G-models were retired from USAF service soon afterwards, leaving just 90 B-52Hs equipping frontline units. Like the B-52Gs, these aircraft are now capable of employing both nuclear and conventional bombs and cruise missiles, and have dropped/fired the latter in combat in Iraq, Kosovo and Afghanistan. Surviving B-52Hs are set to serve until 2040.

B-52H-140-BW Stratofortress 60-0021, 19th BW, Wurtsmith AFB, Michigan, October 1962

SPECIFICATIONS (B-52H)

Crew: Pilot, co-pilot, navigator, bombardier/radar navigator and ECM operator

Length: 160ft 11in (49.05m)

Wingspan: 185ft (56.39m)

Height: 40ft 8in (12.40m)

Empty: 195,000lb (88,450kg)

Max T/O: 505,000lb (229,088kg)

Max Speed: 598mph (957km/h)

Range: 10,059 miles (16,095km)

Powerplant: eight Pratt & Whitney TF33-P-3s

Output: 110,000lb st (4,88kN)

Armament: 60,000lb (27,216kg) of bombs/missiles split between bomb-bay and two underwing stores pylons

First Flight Date: 15 April 1952

B-52G-115-BW Stratofortress 58-0253, 1708th BW(P). King Abdul Aziz AB, Jeddah New, Saudi Arabia, March 1991

PLANE DETAILS

Previous page: This B-52H is armed with GAM-77 Hound Dog cruise missiles, the aircraft regularly flying in this configuration throughout the Cuban Missile Crisis of October/November 1962. The Hound Dog was fitted with a one megaton B28 nuclear warhead and powered by a J52 turbojet engine that gave the weapon a stand-off range of 600 miles. 60-0021 was later converted into a D-21 reconnaissance drone launch platform, and today the aircraft remains in frontline service with the 5th BW at Minot AFB, North Dakota.

This page: Heavily involved in Operation *Desert Storm*, this aircraft performed a single bombing mission from Diego Garcia, in the Indian Ocean, lasting 11.1 hours, before transferring to Jeddah on 17 January 1991. As part of the 1708th BW(P), 58-0253 accumulated a further 214.6 combat flying hours during the course of 52 sorties. Returning to its parent unit (42nd BW) post-war, the veteran bomber was retired to the Aerospace Maintenance and Regeneration Center at Davis-Monthan AFB, in Arizona, in November 1993.

DOUGLAS A-4 SKYHAWK

Bucking the trend for ever larger combat aircraft when built in the early 1950s, the Douglas A-4 was the brainchild of company chief engineer, Ed Heinemann, who had also been responsible for the A-26 and A-1 almost a decade before. Weighing significantly less than half the specified weight (of 30,000lbs) stipulated by the US Navy for its new jet attack bomber, yet still capable of undertaking all the missions required of it, the A4D, as it was designated until 1962, was quickly dubbed 'Heinemann's Hot Rod' thanks to its outstanding performance.

The first A4D-1s entered fleet service in September 1956, and a total of 165 had been built when production switched to the re-engined A4D-2 in 1958. By the time the Vietnam War escalated into all-out conflict in 1965, all carrier air wings included at least two squadrons of Skyhawks. The B-, C- and E-models had all seen the capabilities (and weight) of the A-4 increase since the first examples were built, and the aircraft played a central part in the air war fought by the US Navy and

Marine Corps over Southeast Asia through to 1973. The final operational Skyhawks bought by the US Navy were A-4Fs, 167 of which were acquired in 1967–69. The Marine Corps continued to receive new-build A-4Ms (162 delivered) until 1979, however, this variant equipping frontline light attack units into the 1980s. By then, the US Navy's A-4s were being exclusively used as adversary trainers for fleet fighter units.

The final single-seat Skyhawks (of which 2,405 were built between 1954 and 1979) were retired by the US Navy and Marine Corps in the early 1990s, although export operators Indonesia, Australia, Malaysia, Singapore, New Zealand, Kuwait, Israel and Argentina continued to fly their examples. Two-seat TA-4 trainers soldiered on in US service until 2001, the latter having been built in the 1960s as replacements for the TF-9J Cougar. Some 555 were subsequently constructed for the US Navy/Marine Corps and export markets. Aside from performing intermediate and advanced tuitional roles, TA-4s were also used for FAC, electronic warfare and adversary pilot training.

A-4C Skyhawk BuNo 149574 of VA-153, USS *Coral Sea* (CV 43),
Gulf of Tonkin, March 1965

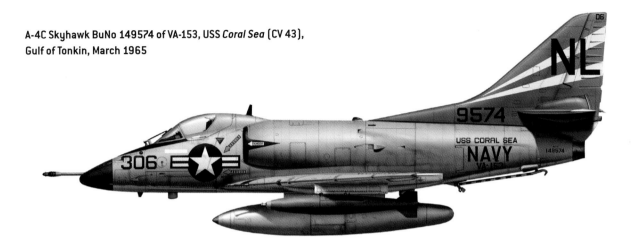

SPECIFICATIONS (A-4E)

Crew: Pilot

Length: 40ft 1.50in (12.22m)

Wingspan: 27ft 6in (8.38m)

Height: 15ft (4.57m)

Empty: 9,284lb (4,211kg)

Max T/O: 24,500lb (11,113kg)

Max Speed: 685mph (1,102km/h)

Range: 920 miles (1,480km)

Powerplant: Pratt & Whitney J52-P-6

Output: 8,500lb st (38kN)

Armament: Two Mk 12 20mm cannon in wing roots; 8,200lb (3,720 kg) of bombs/rockets/ missiles on four underwing/one centre fuselage stores pylons

First Flight Date: 22 June 1954

A-4N Skyhawk '401' of the Flying Dragon Squadron, Nevatim,
Israel, 1988

PLANE DETAILS

Previous page: Armed with Mk 84 2,000lb bombs, and boasting a 300-gallon centreline tank, this aircraft saw considerable action during VA-153's first war cruise to Vietnam. It did not survive this deployment, however, the aircraft being shot down by anti-aircraft artillery north-west of Than Hoa, in North Vietnam, on 25 June 1965 whilst being flown by Carrier Air Wing 15's CO, Cdr Peter Mongilardi. The latter failed to eject from the A-4 and was killed.

This page: Dubbed the Ahit (Eagle) in Israeli service, the A-4 Skyhawk formed the backbone of the Israel Defence Force/Air Force's attack arm from 1966 through to the 1970s. More than 200 aircraft were eventually acquired by the Israelis, who suffered serious losses to their Skyhawk ranks during the 19-day Yom Kippur War in October 1973 (more than 50 A-4s were shot down). This particular aircraft remained in frontline service into the 1990s, flying missions over Lebanon in 1991.

HANDLEY PAGE VICTOR

Designed to meet the same specification (B 35/46) as the Avro Vulcan, the HP 80 Victor was expected to fly so fast and so high that it would be virtually immune to interception. In order to achieve the highest possible cruising Mach number, the wing was designed to what was dubbed a 'crescent' shape by Handley Page engineers, the flying surface being sharply swept but with a thicker inner section to house the aircraft's four Rolls-Royce Sapphire engines. A superb technical achievement, the prototype Victor made its first flight on 24 December 1952.

The last of the RAF's trio of V-bombers to enter service in 1955, the aircraft had taken so long to develop that by the time it reached the frontline it could be intercepted by supersonic fighters or shot down by surface-to-air missiles. Production orders for the Victor were also scaled back to such an extent that the 50 B 1s built were prohibitively expensive. In order to offer better protection to these aircraft, the B 1s were progressively upgraded to B 1A standard through the fitment of better electronic countermeasures (ECM) equipment. Survivors were converted into K 1A tankers in 1965–67 after the nuclear deterrent mission was passed on to the Royal Navy's Polaris missile submarine force.

The more powerful B 2, fitted with Rolls-Royce Conways and boasting a completely redesigned airframe and systems, entered service in the early 1960s, just 34 aircraft being built. These were used in the low-level strike role, carrying the British-built Blue Steel cruise missile. Eight were also modified to carry out strategic reconnaissance missions because the B 2 was then the longest-ranging aircraft in the RAF. Twenty aircraft became K 2 tankers once the nuclear mission was taken over by the Polaris submarines in the late 1960s. These aircraft proved invaluable during the Falklands War in 1982, supporting Vulcan strikes on Port Stanley from Ascension Island, and also during Operation *Desert Shield/Storm* in the Gulf in 1990–91. The last surviving Victor K 2s jets were retired from RAF service on 30 November 1993.

Victor B 2R XH675 of No 100 Sqn, RAF Wittering, Peterborough, 1964

SPECIFICATIONS
(VICTOR B 2)

Crew: Pilot, co-pilot, tactical navigator, radar operator, air electronics operator

Length: 114ft 11in (35.05m)

Wingspan: 120ft (36.58m)

Height: 30ft 1.50in (9.20m)

Empty: 91,000lb (41,277kg)

Max T/O: 233,000lb (101,150kg)

Max Speed: 640mph (1,030km/h)

Range: 4,600 miles (7,400km)

Powerplant: four Rolls-Royce Conway 201s

Output: 82,400lb st (366kN)

Armament: Up to 35,000lb (15,890kg) of bombs/missiles in internal bomb-bay

First Flight Date: 24 December 1952

Victor K 1 XA937 of No 214 Sqn, RAF Marham, Norfolk, 1966

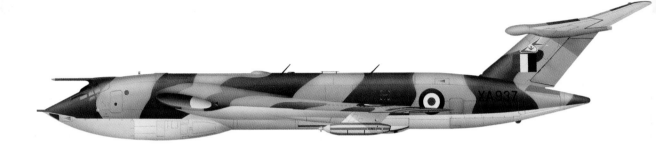

PLANE DETAILS

Previous page: XH675, seen here in all-white finish with an underslung Blue Steel missile, lacks its full ECM aerial fit in this profile. The aircraft left Wittering in October 1968 and joined No 55 Sqn at Marham as a K 2 tanker on 30 March 1977. It moved to No 55 Sqn on 1 October 1980 and was scrapped in December 1993.

This page: XA937 joined No 10 Sqn as a B 1 bomber on 4 June 1958. It later became the first Victor to be converted into a K 1, whereupon it went to No 57 Sqn at Marham on 15 February 1966. The aircraft moved across to No 214 Sqn on 3 October 1966, and it is seen here with the unit's distinctive nightjar in flight insignia on its fin. XA937 retired to St Athan on 7 February 1977.

AVRO VULCAN

One of three jet bombers that formed the RAF's V-Force in the early years of the Cold War, the Vulcan was perhaps the best of the trio. Designed with a wing that was almost a perfect triangle in shape, the Avro 698 prototype possessed fighter-like manoeuvrability at low level despite its size and low-powered Avon engines. The first prototype made its maiden flight on 30 August 1952, while the second prototype was repeatedly rolled at low level during a series of memorable demonstration flights.

The Vulcan entered service in B 1 form in February 1957, production examples differing from the Avro 698 in having a kinked and cambered wing leading edge and more powerful Olympus 101 engines. A total of 45 B 1s and B 1As were built, the latter aircraft being fitted with Olympus 102 or 104 engines of still greater power. The B 1A also had an extended and bulged rear fuselage section filled with ECM equipment.

Some B 1As had refuelling probes installed above the aircraft's huge bombing radar in the nose, and all B 1/1As were delivered to the RAF in anti-radiation white. Further improvements were introduced with the B 2, which was optimised for high altitude performance with thinner wings of greater span and area, as well as 17,000lb st Olympus 201 engines. Most were equipped to carry the Blue Steel stand-off missile, but by 1966 around 50 Vulcans had been repainted in green/grey camouflage, re-engined with 20,000lb st Olympus 301s and redeployed in the tactical low-level bombing role using gravity bombs after the nuclear mission had been taken over by the Royal Navy's Polaris submarine force. Three B 2s saw combat in May–June 1982 during the Falklands War, carrying out what was then the world's longest-range bombing missions. Six months later the last Vulcan bombers were retired. The Falklands conflict had stretched the RAF's aerial refuelling assets to the limit, so it was decided to convert the six best Vulcans still in operational service into K 2 tankers. These were used by No 50 Sqn until 1 April 1984, when the Vulcan was finally retired from RAF service.

Vulcan B 2BS XL317 of No 617 Sqn, Scampton, Lincolnshire, 1963

SPECIFICATIONS
(VULCAN B 2)

Crew: Pilot, co-pilot, tactical navigator radar operator, air electronics operator

Length: 105ft 6in (32.15m)

Wingspan: 111ft (33.83m)

Height: 27ft 2in (8.26m)

Empty: 83,573lb (37,908kg)

Max T/O: 250,000lb (113,398kg)

Max Speed: 640mph (1,030km/h)

Range: 4,600 miles (7,400km)

Powerplant: four Rolls-Royce Olympus 301s

Output: 80,000lb st (358kN)

Armament: Up to 21,000lb (9,525kg) of bombs/missiles in internal bomb-bay

First Flight Date: 30 August 1952

Vulcan B 2 XM648 of No 101 Sqn, Waddington, Lincolnshire, May 1982

PLANE DETAILS

Previous page: This 'Dambusters' Vulcan B 2 wears the unit's 'lightning flash' tail marking in pastel shades and has a full colour squadron badge on the forward fuselage. The aircraft carries a W100A pre-production Blue Steel missile under its belly. The W100A variant lacked a warhead, but otherwise closely resembled the operational W105. XL317 had a long career, serving with a large number of units before ending its days with No 617 Sqn, after which it was retired to become a crash/rescue training airframe at RAF Akrotiri, Cyprus, in 1981.

This page: XM648 was originally delivered to No 9 Sqn in May 1964 and remained with the Coningsby Wing until it moved to Cottesmore. The jet transferred to the Waddington Wing in January 1968 and subsequently served with Nos 101, 44 'Rhodesia' and 9 Sqns – it joined the latter unit in September 1980, and celebrated the Vulcan's 25th anniversary the following year. XM648 was transferred to No 101 Sqn in September 1981, but was withdrawn from service exactly one year later and scrapped at Waddington soon afterwards.

VOUGHT F-8 CRUSADER

The US Navy's first supersonic day interceptor and its last single-engined, single-seat fighter, the Crusader was built in response to a 1952 naval requirement for an aircraft with high-speed performance, but a 115mph landing speed. It achieved the latter through the employment of a unique high-mounted variable incidence wing, which angled up to increase drag – it was also employed during take-off, as it greatly increased lift. One of eight designs submitted to the US Navy, Vought's XF8U-1 prototype made its maiden flight on 25 March 1955, and service deliveries commenced in March 1957.

A total of 318 'Dash Ones' (redesignated F-8As in 1962) were built, and they equipped both US Navy and Marine Corps fighter units. These were followed in 1958 by 130 F8U-1Es (F-8Bs), which featured limited all-weather interception capabilities thanks to the fitment of AN/APS-67 radar. By then the first of 144 F8U-1Ps (RF-8As) had reached the fleet, these aircraft swapping their cannon for five cameras in the forward fuselage. An important reconnaissance asset for the US Navy over the next 25 years, 73 surviving RF-8As were converted into RF-8Gs in 1965–66 – these aircraft had bigger engines, strengthened airframes and improved cameras. The RF-8 saw action over Cuba in 1962 and Vietnam.

The F8U-2 (F-8C) entered service in 1959–60, 187 examples featuring bigger engines and avionics upgrades, after which production shifted to the F8U-2N (F-8D). This aircraft had more armament, a larger engine, more fuel and an improved radar – 152 were built in 1960–62. The last Navy variant was the F-8E, 286 of which were delivered from 1961. This aircraft had improved search and fire-control radar and provision for up to 5,000lb of external stores under the wings. In 1966 Vought commenced a remanufacturing programme that saw 373 Crusaders upgraded to H- and J-models. Although the fighter variant disappeared from US Navy ranks in the mid-1970s, the RF-8 soldiered on until 1987. A small number of second-hand jets were also supplied to the Philippines, and France acquired 42 F-8(FN)s, which it flew from its carriers until 2000.

F-8H Crusader BuNo 147916 of Lt N. K. McCoy, VF-51,
USS *Bon Homme Richard* (CV 31), Gulf of Tonkin, August 1968

SPECIFICATIONS (F-8D)

Crew: Pilot

Length: 54ft 3in (16.53m)

Wingspan: 35ft 8in (10.87m)

Height: 15ft 9in (4.80m)

Empty: 17,541lb (7,957kg)

Max T/O: 29,000lb (13,154kg)

Max Speed: 1,228mph (1,976km/h)

Range: 1,737 miles (2,795km)

Powerplant: Pratt & Whitney J57-PW-20

Output: 18,000lb st (80kN)

Armament: Four Colt 20mm cannon in fuselage; maximum bomb/rocket/missile load of 5,000lb (2,268kg) on two underwing and four fuselage side stores pylons

First Flight Date: 25 March 1955

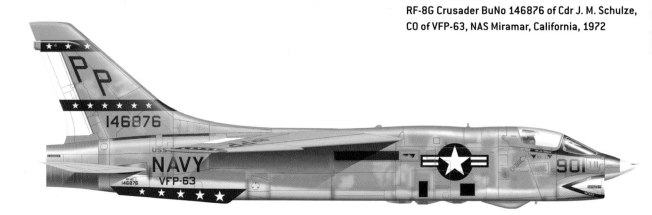

PLANE DETAILS

Previous page: An upgraded D-model, this Crusader was used by Lt Norman McCoy to down a North Vietnamese MiG-21 on 1 August 1968. It appears that the pilot of the downed jet was an eight-victory ace, who successfully ejected. VF-51 completed seven Vietnam deployments with the Crusader, although only one of these saw the unit equipped with F-8Hs.

This page: A veteran of many years of service with the US Navy's photo-reconnaissance community, this aircraft was the first 'photo-bird' lost by VFP-63 during its 'black' period in 1976–77, BuNo 146876 crashing on 1 June 1976. Its pilot, Lt D. Graves, successfully ejected. Between 1 June 1976 and 20 November 1977 VFP-63 lost no fewer than ten RF-8Gs in accidents both on the ground and in the air.

REPUBLIC F-105 THUNDERCHIEF

Conceived by Republic in 1951 as the private venture model AP-63 nuclear strike fighter-bomber that carried its deadly load in a capacious internal bomb-bay, the F-105 Thunderchief which actually entered service seven years later would win fame as a conventional tactical bomber that dropped iron bombs from pylons hung beneath its wings. Flight-testing began with two YF-105As in October 1955, and following technical delays, the first of 75 B-models entered service with the 4th TFW in May 1958. Boasting an all up weight of at least 45,000lb, which made it the biggest single-seat, single-engined combat aircraft in history, the F-105 required the most powerful engine then available. This was the Pratt & Whitney J75 two-shaft afterburning turbojet, which was fitted in all production-standard Thunderchiefs.

Aside from being a big aircraft, the F-105 was also immensely complex, and it took the 4th FW two years to work up with the jet due to further production problems. Indeed, it was not until the advent of the F-105D in 1960 that the jet's fortunes began to improve. This version boasted the General Electric FC-5 fully integrated automatic flight and fire control system, which featured a toss bomb computer, Doppler navigator, missile launch computer, autopilot and search and range radar. Flown by USAF units at home, in Europe and Japan, a total of 610 D-models were built up to 1965. These aircraft would ultimately bear the brunt of the USAF bombing campaign in Vietnam from 1965 through to 1970, undertaking more strikes 'up north' than any other US aircraft. The F-105 units paid a high price in the process, losing 397 jets in combat.

Joining the D-models in Southeast Asia were two-seat F-105Fs, 143 of which had originally been built as trainers in 1963–64. Featuring a lengthened fuselage and taller fin, 61 F-models were modified in 1965–69 to locate, classify and attack enemy ground-based radar sites as electronic warfare F-105G 'Wild Weasels'. Surviving Thunderchiefs were issued to both the Reserve and ANG during the 1960s, and these soldiered on until finally retired in 1984.

F-105D-20-RE Thunderchief 61-0116 of the 562nd TFS/23rd TFW (6235th TFW), Takhli RTAFB, Thailand, 1 September 1965

SPECIFICATIONS (F-105D)

Crew: Pilot

Length: 64ft 3in (19.58m)

Wingspan: 34ft 11.25in (10.65m)

Height: 19ft 8in (5.99m)

Empty: 27,500lb (12,474kg)

Max T/O: 52,546lb (23,834kg)

Max Speed: 1,390mph (2,237km/h)

Range: 2,390 miles (3,846km)

Powerplant: Pratt & Whitney J75-P-19W

Output: 24,500lb st (99kN)

Armament: One M61A1 20mm cannon; maximum bomb/rocket/missile load of 20,000lb (9,072kg) on four underwing and two underfuselage stores pylons

First Flight Date: 22 October 1955

F-105G-1-RE 63-8266 of the 17th WWS/388th TFW,
Korat RTAFB, Thailand, February 1973

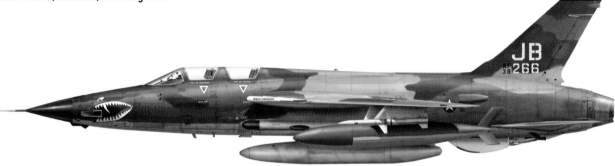

PLANE DETAILS

Previous page: This aircraft is depicted after it had flown 50 combat missions, mostly with the 563rd TFS – the jet still bears the latter unit's markings, as the 562nd's rudder stripes were blue in colour. On 4 December 1965 61-0116 transferred to the 354th TFS/355th TFW at Takhli, and it was lost to flak whilst serving with this unit on 20 July 1966 near Hanoi when Col William Nelson, a senior 355th TFW staff officer, made a second strafing run on a truck. The pilot was killed.

This page: This aircraft was initially accepted as an F-105F on 25 March 1964 for the 4520th CCTW at Nellis AFB. It continued in the training role with the 23rd TFW at McConnell AFB in 1966–67, and then with the 4525th FWW and, in October 1969, the 57th TFW back at Nellis AFB. Converted to F-105G-1-RE configuration by 3 March 1971, 63-8266 flew to Korat RTAFB for service with the 388th TFW until 7 September 1973, when it was reassigned to the 35th TFW.

MIKOYAN MiG-21

The MiG-21 is still very much a frontline fighter type in service across the globe. Indeed, with more than 10,000 examples built in multifarious variants in the former Soviet Union alone (not to mention the improved Chinese F-7 version), the legendary delta-winged design will feature in military circles for a few more years yet. Designed in the aftermath of the Korean War as a day interceptor with the best possible performance, the MiG-21 was developed over a series of prototypes and 40 pre-production aircraft during the mid-1950s. The end result was the definitive MiG-21F-13, which began to enter Soviet service in 1958. This variant was also built in both Czechoslovakia and China.

Later models (there have been at least 14 subsequent variants identified by Western observers) saw the lightweight fighter interceptor developed into a multi-role combat aircraft, boasting more internal fuel, heavier armament and vastly superior avionics. To cope with the increase in all up weight associated with these additions, more powerful 'Soyuz' engines were fitted into the MiG-21. The final variant to enter service was the MiG-21bis, which was essentially the third generation of this famous fighter to reach production. Although now a rarity in Russia, versions of the MiG-21 remain very much frontline equipment in more than 30 countries.

As with previous MiGs, the MiG-21 has seen considerable combat over the past 50 years. Indeed, PF and PFM versions of the aircraft were widely used by the Vietnamese People's Air Force (VPAF) against American strike aircraft and their fighter escorts from 1966. Although the communist pilots initially struggled to come to terms with the fighter's air-search radar and weapons system, the ceaseless cycle of combat operations quickly honed their skills. More than 200 MiG-21 were supplied to the VPAF, and these proved to be formidable opponents for USAF, US Navy and Marine Corps crews through to late 1972. MiG-21s were also fielded in large numbers by Arab air forces in the Middle East, where they suffered heavy losses to Israeli Phantom IIs, Mirage IIIs and Neshers.

MiG-21PF 4324 of Nguyen Dang Kinh, 921st 'Sao Do' Fighter Regiment, Noi Bai, North Vietnam, November 1967

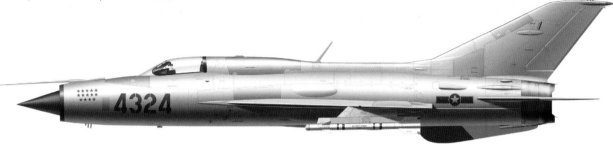

SPECIFICATIONS (MiG-21F)

Crew: Pilot

Length: 51ft 8.5in (15.76m)

Wingspan: 23ft 5.7in (7.15m)

Height: 13ft 6.2in (4.12m)

Empty: 11,795lb (5,350kg)

Max T/O: 20,018lb (9,080kg)

Max Speed: 1,320mph (2,125km/h)

Range: 808 miles (1,300km)

Powerplant: MNPK 'Soyuz' (Tumanskii) R-11F2S-300

Output: 13,613lb st (60.5kN)

Armament: One GSh-23 23mm cannon in centre fuselage; provision for up to 3,307lb (1,500kg) of bombs/rockets/missiles on four underwing stores pylons

First Flight Date: 16 June 1955

MiG-21F-13 5843 of No 26 Sqn, United Arab Republic Air Force,
Sayah-el-Sharif, Egypt, 1969

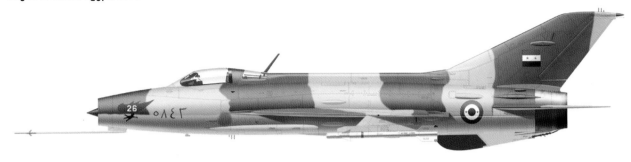

PLANE DETAILS

Previous page: This MiG-21PF enjoyed success with no fewer than nine different pilots whilst serving with the 921st Fighter Regiment in 1967–68, these individuals claiming a total of 14 kills between them. One of the first to claim a victory with the jet was future six-kill ace Nguyen Dang Kinh, who was credited with a share in the destruction of a USAF EB-66 on 19 November 1967 with fellow six-kill ace Vu Ngoc Dinh.

This page: As part of the elite 'Black Ravens' Squadron, this aircraft has the unit's badge sprayed onto its nose. The jet has been carefully painted in a sand and spinach version of the camouflage scheme applied to Egyptian fighters based at Nile Delta airfields after the Six Day War in June 1967. The aircraft's undersides are light blue in colour. The fighter is armed with R-3S missiles on APU-13 launch rails.

McDONNELL DOUGLAS F-4 PHANTOM II

The most famous post-World War II fighter, the McDonnell Douglas F-4 Phantom II is still very much a part of today's military scene, with more than 500 examples being flown by seven air forces across the globe. However, this number is shrinking by the year, with most of the 5,195 built during a 19-year production run having now been retired. Initially designed as an attack aircraft, the jet's role changed to that of a long-range high-altitude fighter in 1955. Powered by two General Electric J79 engines, and featuring a two-crew cockpit, the prototype F4H-1 made its maiden flight in May 1958. By the end of the year the McDonnell design had been selected ahead of the Vought F8U-3 Crusader III as the new US Navy fleet fighter.

Further minor changes were made to the jet to make it more suitable for carrier operations, and deck trials were completed in February 1960. An initial batch of 24 F4H-1 trial aircraft was delivered in 1960–61, and these were redesignated F-4As in 1962. By then the definitive F-4B had begun to enter service with fleet squadrons, the first example having flown on 25 March 1961. The following year a fly-off took place between a US Navy Phantom II and various frontline USAF fighter types, with the results clearly showing that the F-4 was vastly superior to its air force contemporaries. The USAF immediately ordered the aircraft in slightly modified form as the F-4C, and the jet went on to equip 16 of its 23 TAC fighter wings.

The advent of the Vietnam War saw the Phantom II thrust into action, and the design's true multi-role capability soon saw it delivering tons of bombs in large-scale attack formations – photo-reconnaissance RF-4s also played a key role in the conflict. Improved versions of the Phantom II (F-4E and F-4J) made their debut in combat in the late 1960s, whilst foreign customers like Britain, Israel, Germany and Japan all purchased the F-4 in large numbers. The last US Navy F-4Ss were retired in 1987, followed by the Marine Corps in 1990. The USAF kept its Phantom IIs flying until 1996. The aircraft remains in service with Germany, Japan, Iran, Egypt, Turkey, Greece and Israel.

F-4B Phantom II BuNo 153019 of Lt Cdr J. B. Houston and Lt K. T. Moore, VF-51, USS *Midway* (CV-41), Gulf of Tonkin, May 1972

SPECIFICATIONS (F-4J)

Crew: Pilot and radar intercept officer (RIO) in tandem

Length: 58ft 3.75in (17.79m)

Wingspan: 38ft 4.75in (11.72m)

Height: 16ft 3in (4.96m)

Empty: 30,770lb (13,957kg)

Max T/O: 56,000lb (25,401kg)

Max Speed: 1,415mph (2,264km/h)

Range: 1,900 miles (3,040km)

Powerplant: two General Electric J79-GE-10s

Output: 23,940lb st (104kN)

Armament: Up to 16,000lb (7,257kg) of bombs, rockets or missiles on five underwing/fuselage pylons, or in four semi-recessed underfuselage troughs (missiles only)

First Flight Date: 27 May 1958

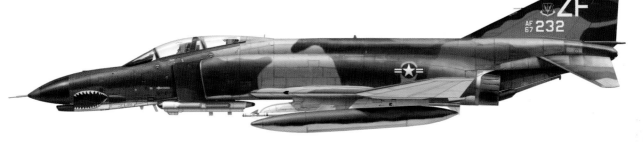

F-4E Phantom II 67-0232 of Capt G. M. Rubus and Capt J. L. Hendrickson, 307th TFS/432nd TRW, Udorn RTAB, Thailand, October 1972

PLANE DETAILS

Previous page: Former F-8 pilot 'Devil' Houston and his RIO Kevin Moore claimed a MiG-17 in this aircraft on 6 May 1972, downing the North Vietnamese jet with an AIM-9 Sidewinder missile. Delivered to the US Navy in December 1962, this veteran aircraft had seen almost a decade of hard frontline service prior to it being transferred to VF-51 in 1971. Subsequently upgraded to F-4N specification in 1973–74, the fighter was eventually retired in the early 1980s and expended as a QF-4N target drone in January 1989.

This page: Captains Rubus and Hendrickson achieved a rare guns kill in this aircraft on 15 October 1972 when they destroyed a MiG-21 with the F-4's M61A1 nose-mounted cannon. Serving with the USAF from June 1968 through to September 1986, 67-0232 was subsequently sold to the Turkish Air Force in October 1987. The aircraft is presently serving with 132 *Filo* at Konya.

DASSAULT MIRAGE III

Conceived to meet the 1952 French Air Force light interceptor specification, the Mirage I was originally powered by two small British Viper turbojets. Dassault had little faith in the concept of low-powered lightweight fighter aircraft, however, and instead decided to develop the larger and heavier Mirage III, powered by an 8,820lb st Atar 101G. The aircraft's most unique feature was its tailless delta configuration, which created reduced drag and allowed the jet to achieve impressive speeds. The prototype Mirage III-001 flew for the first time on 17 November 1956. By the time the first of ten pre-production Mirage IIIAs had started flight testing in May 1958, the new 13,225lb st Atar 9 had replaced the 101G. Thanks to this powerplant, thinner wings and a revised fuselage, the Mirage IIIA-01 became the first aircraft in Western Europe to attain Mach 2 in level flight.

The production standard Mirage IIIC interceptor followed, and the first of 244 was delivered to the French Air Force in July 1961. South Africa and Israel also acquired IIICs, and it was the latter country that gave the fighter its combat debut in 1966. Some 72 Mirage IIICJs were purchased by Israel, and the aircraft enjoyed phenomenal success in aerial combat against a variety of fighter types fielded by neighbouring Arab air arms. Although the Israeli pilots were strapped into Mach 2 fighters, their aircraft lacked any modern radar equipment, leaving them to conduct World War II-style dogfights in jet interceptors.

The improved, multi-role Mirage IIIE fighter-bomber followed several years later, and this variant became the most successful, with 192 operated by the French Air Force, 98 built in Australia (as the Mirage IIIO) for the Royal Australian Air Force, 36 constructed by the Swiss (as the Mirage IIIS) and more than 100 exported to seven other countries. The Mirage IIIR reconnaissance aircraft, which featured cameras in a modified, radarless, nose was also produced in modest numbers for a handful of customers too. Most Mirage IIIs have now been retired, although operational examples remain in service in Pakistan and Argentina.

Mirage IIICJ Shahak 58 of R. Rozen, No 119 Sqn, Tel Nof, Israel, May 1969

SPECIFICATIONS
(MIRAGE IIIE)

Crew: Pilot

Length: 49ft 4in (15.03m)

Wingspan: 27ft (8.22m)

Height: 14ft 9in (4.50m)

Empty: 15,542lb (7,050kg)

Max T/O: 30,205lb (13,700kg)

Max Speed: 1,460mph (2,350km/h)

Range: 1,000 miles (1,610km)

Powerplant: SNECMA Atar 9C-3

Output: 13,670lb st (60.8kN)

Armament: Two DEFA 552A 30mm cannon in lower fuselage; provision for up to 8,818lb (4,000kg) of bombs, rockets or missiles on four underwing and one centreline stores pylons

First Flight Date: 17 November 1956

PLANE DETAILS

Previous page: Pilots flying this aircraft claimed a handful of victories between June 1967 and April 1974. Shahak 58's first two successes were credited to five-victory ace Reuven Rozen. By the time 14.5-victory ace Avraham Salmon claimed the last Shahak double kill while flying this aircraft, the jet was serving with No 101 Sqn.

This page: The Yom Kippur War was in its fourth day when Yehuda Koren used this aircraft to down a Syrian MiG-17. Zvika Vered had also enjoyed success with it three days earlier, claiming a MiG-21 destroyed despite having no afterburner or air-to-air missiles due to technical malfunctions. He downed his MiG with cannon fire.

LOCKHEED SR-71

The ultimate high-speed manned reconnaissance aircraft, the SR-71 was unique in being able to cruise at Mach 3. The aircraft evolved from the CIA-sponsored A-12 programme, which had challenged Lockheed to create a replacement for the company's U-2 spyplane. Under the direction of Clarence L. 'Kelly' Johnson, 18 single-seat A-12s were built in the early 1960s. The short operational career of the A-12 was soon eclipsed by the larger and more capable two-seat SR-71, which was ordered into production by the USAF following flight testing. The first of 31 jets (including three SR-71B trainers) flew on 22 December 1964, and these served exclusively with the 9th Strategic Reconnaissance Wing at Beale AFB, California. Detachments were also maintained at Mildenhall, in Suffolk, and Kadena, on Okinawa.

Flying its first operational sortie – over North Vietnam – on 9 March 1968, this tri-sonic 'hotrod' roamed freely over areas previously denied to the U-2, capturing photographic, radar and electronic intelligence that was used to assess bomb damage and gauge the enemy's order of battle. The SR-71 was also a key asset in intelligence gathering during the Cold War, obtaining information about the Soviet nuclear submarine fleet based in Vladivostok, as well as the port's defences, monitoring the antics of North Korea and flying four 11-hour sorties into the Persian Gulf during the Iran–Iraq War.

An icon of the Cold War, the SR-71 had been in frontline service for almost a decade by the time it started flying from RAF Mildenhall on a regular basis. The aircraft's mission in-theatre was simple – monitor Warsaw Pact troop movements along the Iron Curtain and photograph the ports with access to the Baltic and Barents Seas that were home to the Soviet nuclear submarine fleet. The SR-71 was eventually retired by the USAF in 1990 due to budget cuts, although NASA continued to operate several jets for research purposes. In 1995 two aircraft were briefly brought back into USAF service to plug a gap in US reconnaissance capabilities, but they were permanently retired in 1996.

**SR-71A 64-17974 of the 9th SRW's OL-8,
Kadena AB, Okinawa, September 1968**

SPECIFICATIONS (SR-71)

Crew: Pilot and reconnaissance systems operator

Length: 107ft 5in (37.74m)

Wingspan: 55ft 7in (16.95m)

Height: 18ft 6in (5.64m)

Empty: 60,000lb (27,215kg)

Max T/O: 170,000lb (77,110kg)

Max Speed: 2,012mph (3,220km/h)

Range: 3,018 miles (4,830km)

Powerplant: two Pratt & Whitney J58-1s

Output: 65,000lb st (291kN)

First Flight Date: 22 December 1964

SR-71A '844' 64-17980 of NASA, Edwards AFB,
September 1992 to October 1999

PLANE DETAILS

Previous page: SR-71A 64-17974 Article Number 2025 was the third of three 'Habus' that constituted the first operational deployment of the 9th SRW to Kadena. '974' landed on Okinawa on 13 March 1968 and subsequently notched up OL-8's fourth operational mission – over Vietnam – on 19 April. The aircraft was rotated back to Beale AFB on 16 September, having completed more operational sorties (11) than its two sister aircraft during this six-month milestone deployment.

This page: Following cancellation of the *Senior Crown* programme 64-17980 was loaned to NASA as '844'. On 31 October 1997, the first in a series of experiments began during which '844' flew the Linear Aerospike (LASRE). Three further flights were made before the programme was cancelled in November 1998. 64-17980 made the last flight performed by an SR-71 in October 1999, after which it was put on display at NASA's Hugh L. Dryden Flight Research Facility at Edwards AFB.

GRUMMAN F-14 TOMCAT

Emerging from the failed F-111B fleet fighter programme, the F-14 Tomcat was for many years the world's best long-range defence fighter. Grumman, as lead contractor for the US Navy's version of the F-111, had begun work on the G-303 air defence fighter long before the cancellation of the General Dynamics project, and this was duly selected in January 1969. Built to replace the F-4, the aircraft featured key systems from the F-111B, including the AWG-9 radar, AIM-54 Phoenix missile, TF30 engines and variable-sweep wings. Designated the F-14 by the US Navy, the prototype made its maiden flight on 12 December 1970, and the first of 556 production aircraft reached VF-124 in 1972. VF-1 and VF-2 conducted the first operational deployment with the jet aboard USS *Enterprise* in 1974–75.

The delivery of jets peaked in the early 1980s, by which time 12 Atlantic Fleet and 10 Pacific Fleet units had re-equipped with F-14s, along with single training squadrons on both coasts. The F-14A experienced its first combat in August 1981, when two VF-41 jets shot down two Libyan Su-22s over the Mediterranean – the Libyans would lose two more MiG-23s to VF-32 in January 1989. Selected Tomcat squadrons picked up the photo-reconnaissance mission from the early 1980s following the introduction of the Tactical Air Reconnaissance Pod System, which was carried beneath the fuselage of the jet. Fifty A-models were re-engined and redesignated as F-14B/Ds in the late 1980s and 76 new-build jets delivered. Both the B- and D-models featured the General Electric F110 engine, whilst the F-14D also boasted all-new radar and digital avionics.

With its fighter mission all but disappearing with the end of the Cold War, the Tomcat saw combat in operations *Enduring Freedom* and *Iraqi Freedom* as a precision bomber that was capable of delivering both laser-guided bombs and GPS-guided J-weapons thanks to the addition of a bolt-on targeting pod. The last remaining F-14Ds were retired in 2006. Today, surviving examples of the 79 F-14As sold to pre-revolutionary Iran in the mid 1970s are the only Tomcats still in service.

**F-14B Tomcat BuNo 161433 of VF-11, USS *John F Kennedy* (CV 67),
Arabian Sea, May 2002**

SPECIFICATIONS (F-14A)

Crew: Pilot and radar intercept officer in tandem

Length: 62ft 8in (19.10m)

Wingspan: 64ft 2in (19.54m)

Height: 16ft (4.88m)

Empty: 40,105lb (18,190kg)

Max T/O: 74,349lb (33,724kg)

Max Speed: 1,553mph (2,485km/h)

Range: 2,012 miles (3,220km)

Powerplant: two Pratt & Whitney TF30-P-412s

Output: 41,800lb st (186kN)

Armament: One M61A1 Vulcan 20mm cannon in forward fuselage; up to eight air-to-air missiles on four wing glove and four fuselage stores pylons, or 14,500lb (6,577kg) of bombs

First Flight Date: 12 December 1970

F-14A Tomcat BuNo 160330/3-6032 of the 81st TFS, TFB 8, Iran, 1986

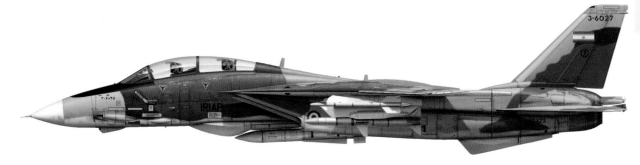

PLANE DETAILS

Previous page: Delivered new to VF-142 in November 1982, this aircraft subsequently became the seventh A-model jet upgraded to F-14A+ specification in the late 1980s. Returned to VF-142, the fighter remained with the unit until it was disestablished in April 1995. 161433 then transferred to VF-103, and three years later it joined VF-11. A veteran of two combat cruises with the 'Red Rippers', the Tomcat went to VF-101 in 2002 and was scrapped on 10 March 2005.

This page: Initially assigned to Tactical Fighter Base (TFB) 7, this aircraft was amongst the first F-14s to be totally overhauled in Iran, and from 1986 it served with TFB 6. In January 1987 3-6032 was used to down an Iraqi Air Force MiG-23. The Tomcat's final fate remains unknown.

McDONNELL DOUGLAS F-15 EAGLE/STRIKE EAGLE

The world's pre-eminent air superiority fighter since its introduction into service in the mid-1970s, the F-15 was the end result of the USAF's F-X requirement launched in the mid-1960s. Embodying lessons learned from air combat in Vietnam, the F-X requirement called for an aircraft that had a thrust-to-weight ratio in excess of unity, and that was able to out-turn any opponent in order to bring its missiles to bear first. McDonnell Douglas' F-15 beat off rival designs and the prototype was first flown on 27 July 1972. Powered by purpose-built Pratt & Whitney F100 turbofans, and featuring the Hughes APG-63 radar, the Eagle was a compelling package.

The first production A-models entered service in January 1976, and 355 single-seat and 57 two-seat F-15Bs were built. Also purchased by Israel, the A-models were upgraded under the Multi Stage Improvement Program in the 1980s. In June 1979 production switched to the F-15C/D, this aircraft initially only featuring moderately improved avionics and equipment, as well as the ability to carry conformal fuel tanks. From February 1983 onwards, C-model jets were subject to the Multi Stage Improvement Program, which saw the Hughes APG-70 radar installed and compatibility achieved with new weapons such as the AIM-120 AMRAAM. Production of the F-15C/D ceased in 1992 following the construction of 622 jets. Examples were exported to Saudi Arabia, Japan and Israel.

Although procured as an air superiority fighter, the F-15 was also designed to field air-to-ground weapons. In May 1984 the USAF chose the F-15E ahead of the F-16XL as a replacement for the F-111. Christened the Strike Eagle, the F-15E featured an APG-70 radar, permanent conformal fuel tanks, improved F100 engines and bolt-on Lockheed Martin targeting pods. The first examples reached the frontline in April 1988, and by mid-1994 204 F-15Es had been delivered. The aircraft made its combat debut in *Desert Storm* in 1991, and has since seen combat in every conflict that the USAF has been committed to. Examples have been exported to Saudi Arabia, Israel, South Korea and Singapore.

**F-15C Eagle 85-0108 of the 58th TFS/33rd TFW,
Tabuk, Saudi Arabia, March 1991**

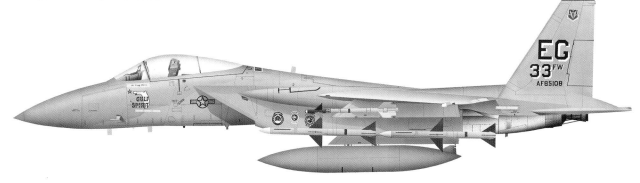

SPECIFICATIONS (F-15C)

Crew: Pilot

Length: 63ft 9in (19.43m)

Wingspan: 42ft 9.75in (13.05m)

Height: 18ft 5.50in (5.63m)

Empty: 28,600lb (12,973kg)

Max T/O: 68,000lb (30,844kg)

Max Speed: 1,678mph (2,685km/h)

Range: 1,228 miles (1,965km)

Powerplant: two Pratt & Whitney F100-PW-220s

Output: 47,660lb st (211kN)

Armament: One M61A1 20mm cannon in right wing root; up to 16,000lb (7,257kg) of missiles in four semi-recessed underfuselage troughs and on three wing/fuselage stores pylons

First Flight Date: 27 July 1972

F-15I Raam 217 of the Hammers Squadron,
Hatzerim, Israel, July 1998

PLANE DETAILS

Previous page: Delivered new to the 33rd TFW in December 1986, this aircraft was credited with the destruction of an Iraqi MiG-23 on 26 January 1991 during Operation *Desert Storm*. It remained with the 33rd until transferred to the 3rd Wing's 12th FS in June 1998, and has since been passed on to the 131st FS of the Massachusetts ANG.

This page: The first export customer for the Eagle, Israel has flown F-15s since 1976. The unrivalled master of the skies in the Middle East, the Israeli Defence Force's F-15A/C force was complemented from 1998 by the awesome two-seat F-15I long-range precision strike fighter/bomber. Based on the USAF's F-15E Strike Eagle, a total of 21 F-15I Raams were acquired.

GENERAL DYNAMICS F-16 FIGHTING FALCON

Developed as the Model 401 in the early 1970s by General Dynamics for inclusion in the USAF's Lightweight Fighter Program, the YF-16 was pitched against designs from four manufacturers. First flown on 20 January 1974, the aircraft beat the rival Northrop YF-17 (forerunner to the F/A-18) in a fly-off that lasted almost a year. The aircraft was chosen to fulfil the USAF's air combat fighter programme requirement, and the first of eight development F-16As performed its maiden flight in December 1976.

Production jets (2,795 A-models would be built for the USAF) began reaching the 388th TFW in January 1979, and aircraft were quickly issued to other fighter wings in the USA, Europe and Asia. Aside from the single-seat jets, the USAF also acquired 204 F-16B two-seaters, which featured full mission avionics and weapons but 17 per cent less fuel. In 1980 the USAF launched the Multi Stage Improvement Program, which it hoped would increase the F-16's multi-role all-weather attack capability through the addition of bolt-on targeting pods. The F-16 would also be made beyond visual range missile-capable. Designated the F-16C/D, production jets started reaching the USAF in late 1984. Fitted with an AN/APG-68 radar in place of the AN/APG-66, the Fighting Falcon (or 'Viper', as it is unofficially known) had improved self-protection jammers and an ability to employ a wider range of munitions.

Subsequent variants also featured larger engines and HARM missile-capability in order to perform the anti-SAM 'Wild Weasel' mission. The US Navy also received 26 stripped-out F/TF-16Ns in 1985–86 to act as adversary trainers. With new F-16Cs entering USAF service, older F-16As were passed onto the ANG and Reserve, and 272 of these were upgraded to Air Defense Fighter standard in the late 1980s so that they could employ AIM-7 Sparrow missiles in defence of the USA. Blooded in combat in *Desert Storm* in 1991, USAF F-16s have seen much combat over the past 20 years. The aircraft has also enjoyed unmatched export success across the globe, and the F-16 remains a key asset in more than 30 air forces.

F-16C Fighting Falcon 92-3920 of the 77th FS/363rd AEW, Prince Sultan AB,
Saudi Arabia, March 2003

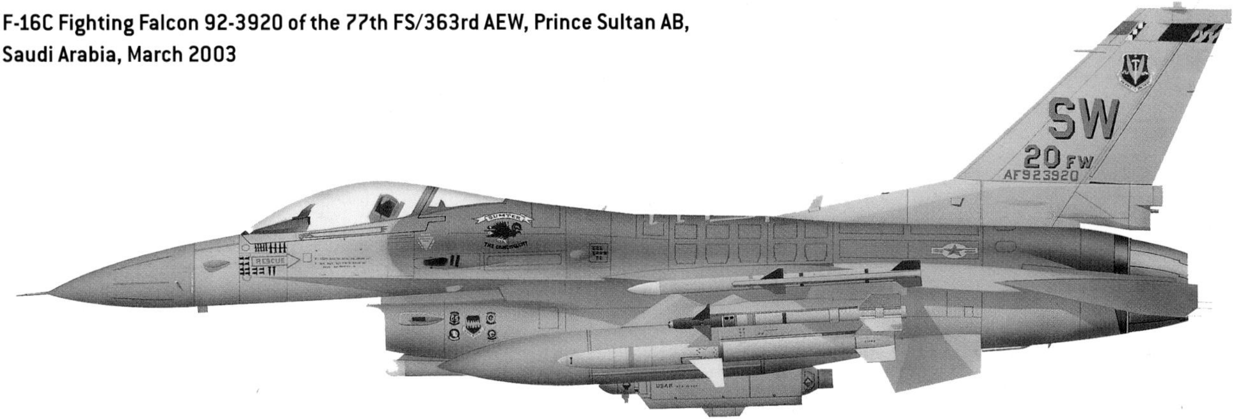

SPECIFICATIONS
(F-16C BLOCK 30/40)

Crew: Pilot

Length: 49ft 4in (15.03m)

Wingspan: 32ft 10in (10m)

Height: 16ft 5in (5.01m)

Empty: 19,100lb (8,665kg)

Max T/O: 42,300lb (19,190kg)

Max Speed: 1,328mph (2,125km/h)

Range: 2,431 miles (3,890km)

Powerplant: General Electic F110-GE-100

Output: 27,600lb st (123kN)

Armament: One M61A1 Vulcan 30mm cannon in
fuselage; provision for up to 12,000lb (5,435kg)
of bombs/rockets/missiles on six underwing,
one underfuselage and two wingtip stores pylons

First Flight Date: 20 January 1974

F-16C Fighting Falcon 88-0416 of the 524th FS/332nd AEW, Al Jaber AB, Kuwait, March 2003

PLANE DETAILS

Previous page: Delivered to the 78th FS in June 1995, this Block 50 jet was then passed on to sister-unit 77th FS and marked up as the flagship of the 20th FW. The aircraft saw considerable action during Operation *Iraqi Freedom*, employing J-weapons, cluster bombs and Maverick missiles as it neutralised surface-to-air missile sites. The fighter remains with the 20th FW today.

This page: An early Block 40 jet, this aircraft was initially assigned to the 34th TFS/388th TFW in August 1989, before being transferred to the 524th TFS in October 1996 when the unit transitioned from F-111s to F-16s. Deployed to Al Jaber in December 2002 in the lead up to Operation *Iraqi Freedom*, the aircraft subsequently flew 22 missions in the conflict. The jet was passed back to the 34th FS/388th FW in 2007, and it is still flown by the unit today.

McDONNELL DOUGLAS F/A-18 HORNET

Following the cancellation of the US Navy's VFAX lightweight multi-role fighter programme in 1974, the US Congress recommended that the navy should focus on a navalised General Dynamics YF-16 or Northrop YF-17, which had been built for the USAF-sponsored Lightweight Fighter project. Neither company had any experience constructing naval aircraft, so McDonnell Douglas paired up with Northrop and Vought went into partnership with General Dynamics. Being twin-engined, the Northrop design had a clear advantage over the YF-16, as the US Navy favours twin-engined aircraft when given the choice.

Selected to develop the YF-17 into a frontline aircraft on 2 May 1975, Northrop and McDonnell Douglas were initially instructed to build separate F-18 fighter and A-18 attack jets. However, these were combined into a single airframe to cut costs, resulting in production of the F/A-18A Hornet. The first of 11 development jets made its maiden flight on 18 November 1978, this machine differing significantly from the YF-17. Bigger and heavier than the latter, the Hornet was powered by two F404 turbofans and featured a Hughes APG-65 radar. It had also been navalised – a strengthened undercarriage and arrestor hook had been fitted and a wing-folding mechanism installed.

Production aircraft reached the navy in May 1980, with the Marine Corps receiving Hornets two years later. A total of 37 1A-models and 40 two-seat F/A-18Bs were delivered to the US Navy/Marine Corps up to 1986, when production switched to the F/A-18C/D. The latter featured improved avionics, a new central computer and greater weapons compatibility, and 464 had been built by the time production ended in 1999. Some 161 of these were two-seat D-models, including 96 night attack jets used by the Marine Corps. In 2002–03 200 F/A-18As were upgraded to A+ specification with C-model avionics. Making its combat debut over Libya in 1986, the Hornet has seen considerable action from carrier decks and ashore. The aircraft also enjoyed modest export success, with seven countries buying F/A-18s.

F/A-18C Hornet BuNo 164045 of VFA-27, USS *Kitty Hawk* (CV 63),
Northern Arabian Gulf, April 2003

SPECIFICATIONS (F/A-18C)

Crew: Pilot

Length: 56ft (17.07m)

Wingspan: 37ft 6in (11.43m)

Height: 15ft 3.50in (4.66m)

Empty: 29,619lb (13,435kg)

Max T/O: 51,900lb (23,541kg)

Max Speed: 1,197mph (1,915km/h)

Range: 2,084 miles (3,335km)

Powerplant: two general Electric F404-GE-402s

Output: 35,550lb st (158kN)

Armament: One M61A1 20mm cannon in nose; 17,000lb (7,711kg) of bombs, rockets or missiles on four underwing, two wingtip (missiles) and one underfuselage stores pylons; two missiles in two semi-recessed underfuselage troughs

First Flight Date: 9 June 1974 (YF-17)

F/A-18D BuNo 164884 of VMFA(AW)-224,
Al Asad, Iraq, January 2005

PLANE DETAILS

Previous page: 164045 was delivered to the US Navy in December 1989 and initially issued to CVW-11's VFA-94. It was transferred to VFA-27 in early 1996 when the latter unit transitioned from 'Alpha' to 'Charlie' model Hornets prior to joining CVW-5 in Japan. The jet was the 'Royal Maces'' CAG 'bird' from mid-1997. Undoubtedly the most colourful Hornet to see combat in *Iraqi Freedom*, this aircraft was passed on to VFA-192 in 2004, and it is still assigned to the unit today.

This page: Built in 1993, this Lot XVI jet was initially delivered to VMFA(AW)-332 and then transferred to VMFA(AW)-533 in 1996. It joined VMFA(AW)-224 in 1997, and has worn this distinctive Bengal Tiger-striped scheme for several years. The jet was involved in VMFA(AW)-224's first bomb-dropping mission in Iraq on 19 January 2005. BuNo 164884 remains assigned to this unit, although it has since lost its tiger stripes.

LOCKHEED F-117 NIGHTHAWK

The end result of the USAF's *Have Blue* programme launched in the mid 1970s, the F-117 was developed by Lockheed's legendary Advanced Development Company – better know as the 'Skunk Works'. The company had been tasked by the USAF to secretly design an attack aircraft that was difficult to detect with radar. Two XST (Experimental Stealth Technology) *Have Blue* prototypes were built, and the first of these flew in December 1977. Similar in appearance to the follow-on F-117, both XSTs were lost in crashes soon after they had been constructed. In November 1978 the green light was given to Lockheed by the USAF to construct the first of five full-scale development aircraft as part of the *Senior Trend* programme. The prototype successfully flew for the first time on 18 June 1981, and the first of 59 production aircraft was delivered to the USAF in August 1982.

Issued to the newly formed, and top secret, 4450th Tactical Group at Tonopah, in Nevada, the unit achieved operational capability in October 1983. The 4450th flew the jet exclusively at night for the first five years of its existence in order retain the veil of secrecy surrounding the F-117A. It also operated a fleet of A-7 Corsair IIs from Tonopah, ostensibly as part of an avionics test programme, so as to legitimise the 4450th's existence. It was not until November 1988 that the F-117A was revealed to the world by the Department of Defense.

The last Nighthawk was delivered to the USAF in mid 1990, and six months later the jet saw combat with the 49th TFG over Baghdad as the group led the opening strikes of Operation *Desert Storm*. The aircraft's faceted airframe construction, radar absorbent material and platypus exhausts, combined with stealthy flight profiles, rendered the F-117 near invisible to enemy radar throughout the campaign. Used in combat since then in the Balkans in 1999 (where one was shot down by a Serbian SAM) and again over Iraq in 2003, the Nighthawk was retired from USAF service in 2008. Most surviving aircraft were placed in storage at Tonopah, although several were placed on display in museums.

F-117A Nighthawk 84-0812 of Capt B. Foley, 415th TFS/37th TFW(P),
King Khalid AB, Saudi Arabia, February 1991

SPECIFICATIONS (F-117A)

Crew: Pilot

Length: 65ft 11in (20.08m)

Wingspan: 43ft 4in (13.20m)

Height: 12ft 5in (3.78m)

Empty: 29,500lb (13,380kg)

Max T/O: 52,500lb (23,815kg)

Max Speed: 650mph (1,040km/h)

Range: 659 miles (1,055km)

Powerplant: two General Electric F404-GE-F1D2s

Output: 21,600lb st (96kN)

Armament: Up to 4,000lb (1,814kg) of bombs/missiles in internal weapons bay

First Flight Date: 18 June 1981

F-117A Nighthawk 88-0841 of Maj R. Shrader, 416th TFS/37th TFW(P),
King Khalid AB, Saudi Arabia, January 1991

PLANE DETAILS

Previous page: 84-0812 has the distinction of flying the most combat missions by an F-117 in Operation *Desert Storm*, the jet completing 42 in total. 84-0812 served with the 49th FW's 7th FS until retired to Tonopah in 2008.

This page: According to Maj Shrader, this aircraft was unpopular with pilots at King Khalid during *Desert Storm* because of its highly sensitive tracker (finger button). Nevertheless, he flew 18 combat missions with it over Iraq and Kuwait. On one of his more memorable sorties, Maj Shrader used 88-0841 to drop a GBU-27 Laser-Guided Bomb on the Iraqi Air Force HQ building, scoring a direct hit. 88-0841 served with the 49th FW's 9th FS until being retired to Tonopah in 2008.

McDONNELL DOUGLAS AV-8B HARRIER II

The world's first practical vertical take-off and landing fixed-wing aircraft, the Harrier was developed from the Hawker P 1127. The jet was powered by the Rolls-Royce Pegasus engine, which was able to vector thrust through 90° from the horizontal via four pivoting exhaust nozzles. Six P 1127s were built to prove the concept, followed by nine Kestrels. Six of the latter were transferred to the USA for testing, and by the late 1960s the Kestrel had evolved into the Harrier.

In 1969 the US Marine Corps placed an order with Hawker Siddeley for 102 single-seat AV-8As and eight two-seat TAV-8As. The Harrier's ability to operate from rudimentary landing sites and the decks of ships (not exclusively aircraft carriers) appealed to the Marine Corps, which needed a strike aircraft to support its beachhead assaults. The first AV-8As arrived in the USA in January 1971, and VMA-513 began work-ups with the jet four months later. Two more frontline squadrons (and a training unit) would swap their F-4s for AV-8s in the next two years. Between 1979–84, 47 AV-8s were upgraded to AV-8C standard, the latter featuring better avionics.

By the time these aircraft had been retired in 1987, McDonnell Douglas and BAe had already started delivering AV-8B Harrier II replacements to the Marines. Similar in configuration to the early AV-8A/C, this aircraft had an enlarged carbon fibre wing, a raised cockpit, lift improvement devices, an uprated Pegasus engine and more weapons pylons. The first of four full-scale development AV-8Bs completed its maiden flight on 5 November 1981, and frontline aircraft began reaching the Marines in January 1984. The two-seat TAV-8B trainer made its first flight in October 1986. A total of 280 AV-8Bs and 27 TAV-8Bs would eventually be acquired by the Marine Corps. The jet made its combat debut in *Desert Storm* in 1991, and since then a considerable number of AV-8Bs have been reworked as night attack Harrier IIs with nose-mounted FLIR or as APG-65 radar-equipped Harrier II(Plus) aircraft. The jets have been heavily committed to operations in Iraq and Afghanistan since 2001.

AV-8B Harrier II BuNo 163663 of VMA-542, King Abdul Aziz AB, Saudi Arabia, November 1990

SPECIFICATIONS (AV-8B)

Crew: Pilot

Length: 46ft 4in (14.12m)

Wingspan: 30ft 4in (9.25m)

Height: 11ft 8in (3.55m)

Empty: 13,968lb (6,336kg)

Max T/O: 31,000lb (14,060kg)

Max Speed: 666mph (1,065km/h)

Range: 2,275 miles (3,640km)

Powerplant: Rolls-Royce F402-RR-408A

Output: 23,800lb st (106kN)

Armament: One GAU-12/A 25mm cannon in underfuselage pod; up to 13,235lb (6,003kg) of rockets, bombs or missiles split between seven underwing/fuselage stores pylons

First Flight Date: 21 October 1960 (P 1127)

First Flight Date: 5 November 1981 (YAV-8B)

AV-8B BuNo 162081 of VMA-231, King Abdul Aziz AB,
Saudi Arabia, February 1991

PLANE DETAILS

Previous page: This aircraft was delivered to VMA-223 on 30 November 1988 as B-138. VMA-542 took over VMA-231's aircraft upon the unit's return from Japan in mid 1990. The jet was repainted in 'grey-on-grey' camouflage at MCAS Cherry Point prior to deploying to Saudi Arabia, and it is shown here in standard *Desert Storm* configuration. The wing, tail and other components of this aircraft were combined with a new fuselage, engine and other parts to create AV-8B Harrier II+ BuNo 165428 in August 2000.

This page: This Harrier II was delivered to VMA-331 as B-30 on 3 July 1985. VMA-231 acquired the jet from VMAT-203 at MCAS Cherry Point during the unit's marathon deployment from Japan to the Middle East in 1990, BuNo 162081 replacing a 'broken' aircraft that had been left behind during the theatre move. 'Shank 09' had yet to be repainted in 'desert greys' when, on 9 February 1991, it was downed by an Iraqi infra-red SAM over central Kuwait. Capt Russ Sanborn ejected and was captured.

ROCKWELL B-1B LANCER

Initially conceived by Rockwell for the low altitude penetration nuclear bomber role and developed for the USAF in response to the latter's Advanced Manned Strategic Aircraft requirement, issued in 1965, the B-1 was selected as a replacement for the B-52 in 1970 after it had seen off rival designs. The first of four B-1A prototypes performed its maiden flight on 23 December 1974, but in June 1977 the project was cancelled by the Carter administration. The bomber was resurrected four years later as part of President Ronald Reagan's rearming programme, and 100 improved B-1Bs were ordered – Strategic Air Command had hoped to acquire 320.

The B-model featured improved avionics and systems, low observable features such as radar absorbent material coatings to the outer fuselage skinning, strengthened undercarriage, fixed air inlets and the all-important APG-164 radar for navigation and terrain following. The core of the aircraft's defensive systems was the Eaton ALQ-161 ECM suite, which proved unreliable in service. The prototype completed its first flight on 18 October 1984, and production jets began reaching the 96th BW in July 1985. All 100 B-1Bs had been delivered by May 1988, just as its primary nuclear strike mission against the USSR disappeared following the collapse of communism in Eastern Europe.

The USAF initially struggled to find a mission for its hugely expensive fleet of B-1s, but in the mid 1990s it commenced the Conventional Mission Upgrade Program, which saw the bomber modified so that it could carry guided and unguided ordnance. Although retaining its nuclear strike capability, the B-1 Lancer (so named in 1990) can now also employ GPS-guided J-weapons and conventional iron bombs. The jet made its combat debut over Iraq during Operation *Desert Fox* in December 1998, and has since seen action over the Balkans in 1999 and during the ongoing Global War on Terror. Some 67 B-1s are currently used in frontline service, with the remaining aircraft having been retired to the Aircraft Maintenance and Regeneration Center, where they are used as spares for operational jets.

**B-1B Lancer 85-0060 of the 34th BS/28th BW,
Ellsworth, South Dakota, 2005**

SPECIFICATIONS (B-1B)

Crew: Pilot, co-pilot and offensive and defensive systems officers

Length: 147ft (44.81m)

Wingspan: 136ft 8.50in (41.67m)

Height: 34ft 10in (10.62m)

Empty: 192,000lb (87,090kg)

Max T/O: 477,000lb (216,360kg)

Max Speed: 828mph (1,324km/h)

Range: 7,495 miles (11,992km)

Powerplant: four General Electric F101-GE-102s

Output: 123,120lb st (548kN)

Armament: Up to 75,000lb (34,020kg) of bombs/missiles in three internal weapons bays

First Flight Date: 23 December 1974 (B-1A)

**B-1B Lancer 86-0108 of the 28th BS/7th BW,
Dyess, Texas, 2005**

PLANE DETAILS

Previous page: The 20th B-1B delivered to the USAF, this aircraft served with the 127th BS/184th BW at McConnell AFB, Kansas, until the wing switched to the aerial refuelling mission in the mid-1990s. It was then passed on to the 34th BS/28th BW, with whom it still serves today. The aircraft was one of three B-1Bs from Ellsworth that participated in Operation *Odyssey Dawn* in support of the uprising in Libya in 2011.

This page: The 68th B-1B accepted by the USAF, 86-0108 has served with various units within the 7th BW throughout its USAF career to date.